LADY HUNTINGDON
AND
HER FRIENDS

Lady Huntingdon
and
Her Friends

Helen C Knight

CountedFaithful

LADY HUNTINGDON AND HER FRIENDS
First published 1853
This edition © Counted Faithful, 2017

COUNTED FAITHFUL
2 Drakewood Road
London SW16 5DT

Website: http://www.countedfaithful.org

ISBN
Book: 978-1-78872-021-2
ePub: 978-1-78872-022-9
Kindle: 978-1-78872-023-6

Contents

Preface

THE beginning of the eighteenth century was marked by spiritual barrenness in England and her colonies. Immorality and scepticism had blighted the moral consciousness of the nation, and cankered the great heart of the church. In place of the vital, sturdy faith of a former day, there seemed only a perverted Christianity, weak, insincere, effeminate, with "a name to live."

But in this evil and desolate hour, there were in secret places the wrestling Jacobs, whose conflicts issued in "newness of life;" and suddenly, strangely as it seemed to men, the electric appeals of Whitefield, and the powerful preaching of the Wesleys, startled the thronging multitudes of London with the awful verities of the world to come. The doctrines of the cross were proclaimed by earnest men, who themselves had felt their saving power; everywhere souls were sunk in the depths of spiritual want, who laid hold of the "living way" of return to their Father's house set before them in the gospel; and multitudes, renouncing the pomps and vanities of this life, confessed themselves "strangers and pilgrims on the earth," and "desired a better country, that is, an heavenly."

We have singled out from this great company a noble Christian Woman, whose name is blended with the history of this period; whose soul glowed with a fervent faith; and whose princely mansions were open with a tireless hospitality to everyone who loved her Lord. As we follow her path, Wesley goes out from us to stamp his intrepid spirit upon the organism of one of the largest bodies of Protestant Christians, and at some future day we hope to follow him in his career.

Never, perhaps, since the days of the apostles, did the brave, loving, and rejoicing spirit of the gospel more strikingly manifest itself. It embraced the high and the low, the rich and the poor, who, when imbued with its divine life, became *one* in Christ Jesus, members of the same household of faith. In them the new birth was something more than a theological dogma, or an article in the creed; it was a living reality: they rejoiced and testified that they were born of God, for "old things had passed away, all things had become new." Religion no longer consisted in a formal assent to a dead orthodoxy, but it was the life of God in the soul, the living Christianity of the Bible, which is alone transforming and vital.

It is well to study the spiritual development of a period so marked as this – the very period of the great revival of the work of God in America in connection with the labours of Edwards, Brainerd, and the Tennants – in order that we may see clearly the distinguishing elements of the renewed soul: *hatred of sin, love to the Redeemer, and flowing from these, love and good-will to man.* It will help to settle the solemn question, which we doubt not rises upon many a disquieted soul, both within and without the visible church, "Am I really a child of God?" The question returns, Do you honestly and heartily desire to be free from the corruption which underlies your nature, and which makes you an alien from your Father's house? Does your heart go out in tenderness and love to Him who hath borne your iniquities, and by whose stripes you are healed? And with this love in your soul, is it your heart's desire and prayer to God to bear your part, humble though it be, to bring others to this Saviour of lost men? For *this is the fruit of faith.*

Such endeavours may be noiseless, quiet, domestic in their nature, like Harlan Page's, and like many a godly mother's; but they must exist, for the church of Christ is essentially aggressive: its mission is not only to love, but to conquer by love. And while the believer should win a hearing by the purity and blamelessness of his life, the singleness of his aim, and the beauty of his holiness, shall he not "*go forth* bearing precious seed," be ready to "do good and to communicate;" and in humble imitation of his heavenly Master, distribute the living bread, and pour out the healing waters of salvation to famished ones all along the way-sides of life?

1
Natural and Spiritual Birth of Lady Huntingdon

A LITTLE girl is following her playmate to the grave; the funeral badges, the solemn pomp of the procession, the falling of the turf upon the coffin, with the mournful echo, "Earth to earth, ashes to ashes, dust to dust," fill her with profound awe. Death and life seem strangely blended; the great hereafter rises before her amazed and startled vision. Her young heart is bowed. "Oh God, be *my* God, when my hour shall come!" is her anxious though unuttered cry. The impressions of this hour were never lost; neither the bright promises which dawned upon her girlhood, nor their brighter realisation in a brilliant and happy marriage, could ever lull the unrest of her awakened spirit, or silence the cravings of her famished soul. She felt herself in a far country, a wanderer from her Father's house, and she began to be in want.

This child, called *Selina Shirley*, second daughter of Earl Ferrars, was born in Chartley, August 24, 1707. Almost from infancy, an uncommon seriousness shaded the natural gladness of her childhood; in the clear depths of her penetrating eye, and in the curve of her thin lip, were traces of earnest thought, and thought inspired not so much by the sweet solitude and breezy melodies of the grand old trees around her father's mansion, or the ivied ruins of Chartley Castle, or the storied associations of her own ancestral history, as by other and far deeper things. She loved to visit the grass-grown grave of her departed friend, and would often stray to a little closet in her own room, where, screened from the notice of her sisters, she poured out her heart in supplication to the Author of her being. Without any positive religious instruction, for none knew the inward sorrows of this little girl, nor were there any around her who could have led her to the balm there is in Gilead, Selina devoutly and diligently searched the Scriptures, if haply she might find that precious something which her soul craved. That there was a higher good, a purer joy, a loftier love, she was well assured, for her religious instincts kept climbing upward for light and warmth; but where could they be found?

At the age of twenty-one, she was married to Theophilus, Earl of Huntingdon, a man of high and exemplary character, and by this connection became allied to a family whose tastes and principles happily coincided with her own.

Both by birth and by marriage Lady Huntingdon was introduced to all the splendours and excitements of high English life. At the residence of her aunt, Lady Fanny Shirley, at Twickenham, which formed one of the literary centres of that day, and whose mistress was a reigning beauty of the court of George I, she mingled freely with the wits, poets, and authors, then distinguished in the walks of English literature. Among her friends might be numbered the famous Duchess of Marlborough, whose talents were only equal to her temper; Lady Mary Wortley Montague, whose intimacy and quarrels with Pope, as well as her eccentricities, have sent her name down to posterity; Margaret, daughter of the Earl of Oxford, a patroness of literature and friend of Miss Robinson, afterwards the beautiful and accomplished Mrs Montague.

The gifts and graces of the young Lady Huntingdon fitted her to shine in the most elegant circles of England; but whatever she might have been as a leader of fashion, or an actor in political intrigues, or the friend of literary merit, her life comes down to us linked with the Redeemer's cause, and her name is enrolled among those who have loved and laboured for their Lord.

During the first years of her married life, Lady Huntingdon's chief endeavour, amid the shifting scenes of town and country life, was to maintain a conscience void of offence. She strove to fulfil the various duties of her position with scrupulous exactness; she was sincere, just, and upright; she prayed, fasted, and gave alms; she was courteous, considerate, and charitable; at Donnington Park, Ashby de la Zouch, in Leicestershire, the elegant summer residence of the Earl, she was the Lady Bountiful of the neighbourhood; she struggled against infirmities within and temptations from without, and strove to model her outward and inward life after the divine pattern – yet, was Lady Huntingdon happy? The consciousness of seeking to live a virtuous and God-fearing life braced her moral powers and quickened her intellect; but where was the faith that could emancipate her soul from the fear of God's inquisition? "I have done virtuously," was the complacent suggestion of self-love; "but how can I tell when I have done enough?" was the doubtful inquiry of conscience.

So passed the early years of Lady Huntingdon's life; children were born, mingling their lights and shadows in the stately household; no earthly good was withheld, nor were earthly blessings abused by riot or excess; dignity, sobriety, and refinement presided over the homes and halls of the Earl. Among the women of her day it might have been said of his wife, "She excelled them all," yet her heart knew its own sorrows; it was laden with its own hidden burdens.

Lord Huntingdon had several sisters whose thoughtful cast of mind made them particularly welcome to his house. In them, Lady Huntingdon had found kindred spirits; but now came Lady Margaret from Ledstone Hall, bearing a new and rich experience. She was the same Margaret of old, and yet another. Yorkshire and Ledstone, among other towns in Yorkshire, had been "blessed by the labours of a mighty *man of God*. He preached the great doctrines of the cross under a profound and thrilling sense of their value. He went from town to town, from hamlet to hamlet, and house to house, preaching repentance toward God, and faith toward our Lord Jesus Christ." Men paused and listened to his messages; the clergy were woken from their spiritual slumbers, some to receive a new quickening from his words, others to upbraid and drive him from their churches. The sisters of Ledstone Hall heard of his fame, and hungered for the living manna. Mr Ingham was invited to the Ledstone church. The preacher's words fell upon good ground. His simple yet searching appeals alarmed the conscience and melted the heart. Margaret Hastings embraced the truth as it is in Jesus: it was no longer the Christianity of creed and ritual, but a new birth into Christ's spiritual family, with the conscious heirship to a heavenly inheritance.

With this fresh life in her soul, she visited the house of the Earl. What a new world of hopes, of aims, of privileges could she unfold to Lady Huntingdon – pardon through a crucified Saviour – peace such as the world could neither give nor take away; and as she spoke one day, these words fell from her lips: "Since I have known and believed in the Lord Jesus Christ for salvation, I have been as happy as an angel." A believer's blessed testimony, but it found no response in Lady Huntingdon's heart. Margaret's language was like an unknown tongue. It was the report of a strange land. There was no answering tone. She felt herself an utter stranger to those sweet assurances which had hushed the disquiet of her sister's soul, and admitted to the groping spirit a gleam of light from the heavenly world.

Lady Huntingdon was alarmed. Could she, religious from her youth up, be really ignorant of the true way of acceptance with God? Had she not always been doing, struggling? Yet in spite of all, a conviction of shortcoming pressed upon her; and she added austerities and rigors to subdue her sense of indwelling sin.

Alas, she felt only more keenly, that every attempt to make her life answer to the requirements of God's righteous laws, only widened the breach between herself and the Lawgiver. She beheld herself more and more a spiritual outcast. Thus harassed by inward conflicts, Lady Huntingdon was thrown upon a sick-bed, and after many days and nights seemed hastening to the grave. The fear of death fell terribly upon her.

"It was to no purpose," says one of her at this period, "that she reminded herself of the morality of her conduct. In vain did she recall the many encomiums passed upon her early piety. Her best righteousness, so far from justifying her before God, appeared only to increase her condemnation."

There she lay, with every alleviation which the best skill and the tenderest nursing could impart, but there was a malady of the soul which these could not reach. Was there no balm in Gilead, and no Physician there? Then it was that the words of Lady Margaret came laden with wonderful meaning. "I too will wholly cast myself on Jesus Christ for life and salvation," was her last refuge; and from her bed she lifted up her heart to God for pardon and mercy through the blood of his Son.

With streaming eyes she cast herself on her Saviour: "Lord, I believe; help thou mine unbelief." Immediately the scales fell from her eyes; doubt and distress vanished; joy and peace filled her bosom. With appropriating faith, she exclaimed, "My Lord, and my God!" From that moment her disease took a favourable turn; she was restored to health, and what was better, to "newness of life."

Exemplary as Lady Huntingdon had been as a wife and mother, and free from the corruptions of fashionable society, no one could fail to see the transforming influence which grace had wrought in her. Love and self-abasement mellowed the sterner traits of her character; the strong sympathies of her heart gushed out towards the people of God, and henceforth, "My God, I give myself to thee," became the watchword of her life.

At the period of Lady Huntingdon's marriage, there was a little band of students in the bosom of Oxford University who, by prayer and fasting and a rigid self-denial, had laid hold upon the great doctrines of the gospel, and were wrestling with them, like one of old, for a heavenly benediction. Shocked by the scoffing tone and degraded aims of their fellows, and disgusted with the prevailing shallow piety of the pulpit and the church, they asked, "Is there not something holier and loftier than this in the gospel of Jesus Christ?" "Can it not redeem from sin and exalt by the power of an endless life?" Profoundly earnest, they accepted the Bible in its integrity, without abatement or addition, as the charter of their liberties and a missive charged with terrible meaning from God to a fallen world. They gave themselves to the service of the Lord with their whole hearts; nor is it strange, in that period of scepticism and levity, that their devout and steadfast adherence to religious convictions provoked the frowns of their masters, and the ridicule of their companions; but taunts and revilings could not daunt the spirit of such men as Whitefield, the Wesleys, and their more immediate co-partners. Rich in that grace which the Father of our spirits vouchsafes to the waiting and believing followers of his Son, the time came when every corner of England thrilled with the fervid eloquence of their preaching.

After leaving Oxford, Whitefield at Bristol, Ingham in Yorkshire, and Wesley at London, began those fearless and awakening appeals which quickened the vitality of English Christianity, reasserting its demands upon the moral consciousness of the nation.

The Wesleys with Ingham went to Georgia, where, after labouring two years with success ill-proportioned to their zeal, they returned to England. On the voyage and during their stay, having been thrown into the society of some Moravian missionaries, whose simple piety won their confidence and love, they lost no time on their arrival at London in visiting the Moravian chapel at Fetter's Lane, where Wesley's career properly begins, but whence he not long after withdrew to lay, as it seemed, not only the foundations of a new encampment in the great Christian army, but to give urgency and a name to that religious renovation which the church needed, both to maintain her supremacy, and to quicken her onward march in the conquest of the world.

As Margaret Hastings, from whose lips she first heard the joyful language of a saving faith, was a disciple of Ingham, no wonder that when Lady Huntingdon experienced its blessed effects in her own soul, she turned from the more frigid and formal teaching of former spiritual guides with a yearning heart towards the new. On her recovery, she sent for John and Charles Wesley, then in London, to come and visit her, expressing a warm interest in their labours, and bidding them God speed in the great and glorious work of urging men to repentance and to heaven. This was in the year 1739, and Lady Huntingdon was at the age of thirty-two.

In Lady Huntingdon they found an ardent friend, and a fearless advocate of their new movements. To her, new movements wore no portentous look when the church was sleeping at her post, and the world around was sinking to ruin. The vigorous itinerant preaching which constituted the then new, though revised instrumentality for meeting the wants of the time, whether among the colliers of Kingswood, the London rabble on Kennington Common, or the farmers of the Yorkshire dales, strongly contrasted with, and boldly rebuked the stagnant ministrations of the sporting clergy, the grave decorum of their more serious brethren, and the utter indifference generally felt about providing suitable means of moral culture for the great masses of half-savage workmen living in the principal cities of the kingdom.

Both the Earl and his wife became frequent attendants upon the ministry of Wesley; and while Lady Huntingdon took great delight in the society of her new Christian friends, she did not neglect to urge upon her former associates the claims of that gospel which she had found so precious to her own soul. The rebuffs which she sometimes met with on these occasions form a curious page in the chapter of human pride.

"The doctrines of these preachers are most repulsive," writes the proud Duchess of Buckingham, "and strongly tinctured with impertinence and disrespect towards their superiors, in perpetually endeavouring to level all ranks and do away with all distinctions. It is monstrous to be told that you have a heart as sinful as the common wretches that crawl upon the earth. This is highly offensive and insulting, and I cannot but wonder that your ladyship should relish any sentiments so much at variance with high rank and good breeding."

"Your concern for my religious improvement is very obliging," thus discourses the unhappy Lady Marlborough; "God knows we all need mending, and none more than myself. I have lived to see great changes in the world – have acted a conspicuous part myself – and now hope in my old age to obtain mercy from God, as I never expect any at the hands of my fellow-creatures. Good, alas, I do want; but where among the corrupt sons of Adam am I to find it? Your ladyship must direct me. But women of wit, beauty, and quality cannot bear too many humiliating truths – they shock our pride. Yet we must die – we must converse with earth and worms. I have no comfort in my own family, and when alone my reflections almost kill me, so that I am forced to fly to the society of those whom I detest and abhor. Now there is Lady Frances Sanderson's great rout tomorrow night; all the world will be there, and I must go. I do hate that woman as much as I hate a physician; but I must go, if for no other purpose but to mortify and spite her. This is very wicked, I know, but I confess my little peccadillos to you; your goodness will lead you to be mild and forgiving."

This, then, is the bitter experience of one who had been the companion of princesses and the ornament of courts; "vanity and vexation of spirit." It tears away the trappings of wealth and station, and startles us by a sight of the bad passions which lie cankering beneath. Let it be contrasted with the freshness and beauty of the believer's life.

"What blessed effects does the love of God produce in the hearts of those who abide in him," writes Lady Huntingdon to Charles Wesley. "How solid is the peace and how divine the joy that springs from an assurance that we are united to the Saviour by a living faith. Blessed be his name. I have an abiding sense of his presence with me, notwithstanding the weakness and unworthiness I feel, and an intense desire that he may be glorified in the salvation of souls, especially those who lie nearest my heart. After the poor labours of the day are over, my heart still cries, 'God be merciful to me a sinner!' I am deeply sensible that daily, hourly, and momentarily I stand in need of the sprinkling of my Saviour's blood. Thanks be to God, the fountain is always open; O what an anchor is this to my soul!"

2

A Glance at Familiar Faces

AMONG Lady Huntingdon's friends and guests we find dear, familiar and honoured names. Behold that little feeble old man, shy in manner, yet rich in speech: bodily infirmity has long beset his path, and driven him from public and stirring life to the retirement which he dearly prized. For him the country had manifold charms, and thus he sings:

> "I search the crowded court, the busy street,
>   Run through the villages, trace every road.
> In vain I search; for every heart I meet
>   Is laden with the world, and empty of its God.
>
> How shall I bear with men to spend my days?
>   Dear feathered innocents, you please me best;
> My God has formed your voices for his praise,
>   His high designs are answered by your tuneful breast."

Wherever he goes, he is regarded with veneration and love, for his mind is stored with knowledge and his heart is alive with tender sympathies. He is the author of many a learned treatise, a father in the ranks of nonconformity, and has a fame both in the Old World and the New; yet we know and love him best as author of the sweet cradle-song, "Hush, my dear, lie still and slumber," which lulled us to sleep in the nursery, and of those psalms and hymns which are destined to shape the experience and lead the worship of millions, when the fame of his learning shall no more be remembered.

This is *Dr Isaac Watts*, the venerable pastor at Stoke Newington. He was born in the stormiest days of nonconformity, and we find him nursed in the arms of his sorrowing mother on a stone by the prison walls which confine his father, a "godly man and a deacon," willing to suffer constraint and persecution for conscience' sake. He is without the endearing treasures of wife and children, for he was never married; "yet his lines have fallen to him in pleasant places and he has a goodly heritage," for he is the beloved and honoured member of a family "which, for piety, harmony, order, and every virtue, was a house of God;" here were "the retired grace, the fragrant bower, the spreading lawn, the flowery garden," with comfort, elegance, friendship, and books.

"I came to the house of this my good friend Sir Thomas Abney, intending to spend a single week beneath his roof," said Dr Watts one day, "and I have extended my visit to thirty years."

"I consider your visit, my dear sir," responded Lady Abney, "as the shortest my family ever received." Sir Thomas, Alderman of London, a pious and exemplary man, whose dignities did not seduce his heart from his God, died in 1722, eight years after Watts had come under his hospitable roof. The mournful occasion was commemorated by an elegiac from the poet-pastor; closing with a note of praise, always so congenial to his spirit:

> *"Great God, to thee we raise our song –*
> *Thine were the graces that enriched his mind;*
> *We bless thee that he shone so long,*
> *And left so fair a track of pious life behind."*

After Sir Thomas' death, he still remained in the family, an honoured and cherished member of the fireside circle.

Dr Watts was settled at Stoke Newington in 1702; the extreme delicacy of his health prompted his people the next year to associate with him Rev Samuel Price. The love he bore to his charge, and the high estimate he entertained of the relation which bound him to it, is thus touchingly expressed: "I pronounce it with the greatest sincerity," said he, "that there is no place or company or employment this side of heaven, which can give me such a relish of delight as when I stand ministering holy things in the midst of you." Nor was it from the pulpit that his influence was chiefly exercised: whenever his health permitted, his pastoral visits from house to house were kind, instructive, and edifying; while a fifth, or as some say, a third part of his income was spent in charities.

There were then no associations, as now, to circulate the Word of life at home and abroad. Bible, Missionary, and Tract societies were the growth of a later day, nay, the product of that very renovation of English Christianity which was then in progress. "I sometimes regret foolishly enough," said Hannah More, "while assisting in the formation and watching the growth of the religious institutions which have so distinctly marked the present century, that some of my earliest and dearest friends did not live to promote and rejoice in them." Nor can we help thinking how both Watts and Doddridge would have rejoiced in those things which we now see and hear, when the knowledge of the Lord is so fast filling the earth.

"I have long been in pain," wrote Colonel Gardiner to Doddridge, "lest that excellent person, Dr Watts, should be called to heaven before I had an opportunity of letting him know how much his works have been blessed to me, and of course of returning to him my hearty thanks. I must beg the favour of you to let him know that I intended to have waited on him in the beginning of last May, when I was in London; but was informed, and that to my great sorrow, that he was extremely ill, and therefore that I did not think a visit would be seasonable. I am well acquainted with his works, especially with his psalms, hymns, and lyrics. How often, by singing some of these to myself on horseback and elsewhere, has the evil spirit been made to flee away:

> *"Whene'er my heart in tune was found,*
> *Like David's harp of solemn sound.*

"I desire to bless God for the good news of his recovery; and entreat you to tell him, that although I cannot keep pace with him here in celebrating the high praises of our glorious Redeemer, which is the great grief of my heart, yet I am persuaded, when I join the glorious company above, where there will be no drawbacks, that none will out-sing me there, because I shall not find any that has been more indebted to the wonderful riches of divine grace than I.

> *"'Give me a place at thy saints' feet,*
> *On some fallen angel's vacant seat,*
> *I'll strive to sing as loud as they*
> *Who sit above in brighter day.'"*

Lady Huntingdon had the pleasure of introducing these two men to each other; and we can almost see the tall and stately figure of the colonel, dressed in his regimentals, bending with love and veneration before the feeble and palsied poet, seemingly more attenuated by his closely fitting breeches and skull cap. What a whole-souled heartiness in the soldier's grasp! How affectionate and sympathising is the answering pressure of the old man's hand!

Colonel and Lady Frances Gardiner were frequent guests of Lord Huntingdon, during their visits in London.

"And I cannot express," exclaimed Lady Huntingdon, "how much I esteem that most excellent man Colonel Gardiner. What love and mercy has God shown in snatching him as a brand from the burning! He is truly alive to God, and pleads nothing but the plea of the publican, 'God be merciful to me a sinner.' What a monument of his mercy, grace, and love! To glorify God and serve him with all his ransomed powers is now his only aim."

Behold another, one whom Dr Watts tenderly loves: he is a young man of tall and slender make, whose sincerity and sweetness of manner win our confidence and bespeak affection. You hear him talk, and everything he says bears the aroma of deep and genuine piety; nothing dogmatic or uncharitable or censorious falls from his lips; his spirit is not fettered by denominational barriers, but he recognises his Master's image and embraces his Master's followers, as well within the pale of the stately English church, and among the rude tenants of Moorfields, as among the stern believers belonging to his own household of faith. He is the popular preacher, and successful teacher, *Philip Doddridge* of Northampton.

When it was proposed to establish a college among the dissenters, Doddridge, then quite young, was requested to express his views upon the best method of preparing young men for the ministry. He drew up a paper, which was sent to Dr Watts for his opinion. Much pleased with the breadth and soundness of the article, the doctor immediately opened a correspondence with the young author, expressing a hope that he might one day be able to carry his admirable plan into execution. He was already a favourite and rising preacher: soon after completing his studies, he received an urgent call to settle over a large dissenting congregation in London; this, with other flattering invitations, he refused, preferring the humble parish of Kibworth, with less hurry and more leisure for study and self-improvement. To some of his friends, who seemed to pity his obscure fortunes, he thus beautifully replies:

"Here I stick close to those delightful studies which a favourable Providence has made the business of my life. One day passeth away after another, and I only know it passes pleasantly with me. I live like a tortoise shut up in its shell, almost always in the same town, the same house, and the same chamber; yet I live like a prince – not indeed in the pomp of greatness, but the pride of liberty – master of my books, master of my time, and I hope I may add, master of myself. I can willingly give up the charms of London, the luxury, the company, and the popularity of it, for the secret pleasures of rational employment and self-approbation, retired from applause or reproach, from envy and contempt, and the destructive baits of avarice and ambition; so that instead of lamenting it as my misfortune, you should congratulate me upon it as my happiness, that I am confined to an obscure village, seeing it gives me so many valuable advantages to the most important purposes of devotion and philosophy, and I hope I may add, usefulness too."

Behold the sweet contentment of the village pastor, at rest with himself and happy in his God: no ambitious cravings, no secret repinings, no envious comparisons, no feverish excitements, disturb the peaceful flow of his devout and useful life. But at Kibworth, Doddridge was not destined to remain; the Lord had other work for his servant. Unknown to himself, he was preparing for him a fame as wide as the Christian world.

In 1729, he received a pressing call to an important dissenting congregation at Castle Hill, Northampton. Various circumstances conspired, which caused his best friends to urge his accepting it. He did so; and in addition to his pastoral and pulpit duties, he established an academy for young men upon the plan already mapped out, which had received the universal approbation of his ministerial brethren. Doddridge is now twenty-eight years old.

A life-work was before him, and he entered upon it with an elastic and bounding spirit – more than that, with systematic and steady diligence. At the beginning of every year he laid out an exact plan of business, as also for every month, week, and day, so that the work of today should not clash with that of tomorrow; and he continued to have a few hours every week, to which no particular business was allotted. These he set apart as a sort of surplus capital, out of which he might repair his accidental losses, or be enabled to meet, now and then, some unexpected call. "It seems to me," he says, "that activity and cheerfulness are so nearly allied, that we can hardly take a more effectual method to secure the latter, than to cultivate the former, especially where it is employed to sow the seed of an immortal harvest."

Yet, with all his weightier cares, the humblest of his flock found access to him, and he could turn away pleasantly from his most favourite studies to hear their sorrows, to comfort, and to counsel them. In short, his life abounded with those "sweet courtesies" which his kindly nature no doubt rendered easy to him, but which he never ceased to cultivate in himself or commend in others.

"I know that these things are mere trifles in themselves," saith he, "but they are the outguards of humanity and friendship, and effectually prevent many a rude attack, which, though small, might end in fatal consequences."

"And as a husband," he says, "may I particularly avoid everything which has the appearance of pettishness, to which, amidst my various cares and labours, I may in some unguarded moment be liable. May it be my daily care to keep up the spirit of religion in conversation with my wife, to recommend her to the divine blessing, and to manifest an obliging and tender disposition towards her; and as a father, may it be my care to intercede for my children daily, to endeavour to bring them early to communion with the church, and to study to oblige them and secure their affections."

But busy as the preacher, the pastor, and the father must now be, Dr Watts singled him out to do a work which it had long been one of his own chief desires to execute, but which his increasing infirmities now warned him to relinquish. It was to prepare a small volume upon practical and experimental religion for popular use.

"In the doctrines of divinity and the gospel of Christ, I know not any man of greater skill than himself," says the doctor of his friend and favourite, "or hardly sufficient to be his second, as he hath a most exact acquaintance with the things of God and our holy religion, and he hath a most happy manner of teaching those who are younger. He is a most affectionate preacher and pathetic writer; and in a word, since I am now advanced in age, beyond my seventieth year, if there were any person to whom Providence would suffer me to commit a second part of my life and usefulness, Doddridge would be the man;

besides all this he possesseth a spirit of so much charity, love, and goodness towards his fellow-Christians who may fall into some lesser differences of opinion, as becometh a follower of the blessed Jesus."

Doddridge declined the work on account of his manifold duties, until he dared no longer to resist the urgency of his venerable friend. He consented to undertake it, and in 1745 the book was issued, dedicated to Dr Watts, and called, "*The Rise and Progress of Religion in the Soul.*" The gratified doctor pronounced it a most excellent performance, "its dedication being the only thing he felt disposed to find fault with." The little book has preached all over Christendom: today it is telling the story of the cross in ten thousand homes, and multitudes, we may well suppose, like Wilberforce and Stonehouse, have reason to bless God for its searching appeals.

At the advent of Wesley and Whitefield, the interests of genuine piety seem to have been at as low an ebb among the dissenting churches as among the Episcopal, though in each there were beacon-lights on the black shores of indifference and scepticism. If Burnet could grievously exclaim, "When I see the gross ignorance of those who apply for ordination, and the want of piety and scriptural knowledge in those already in the sacred office, these things pierce my soul and make me cry out, 'Oh, that I had wings like a dove, for then would I fly away and be at rest.' What are we likely to grow to? How are we to deal with adversaries, or in any way promote the honour of God and carry on the great concerns of the gospel, when, in the fundamentals of religion, those who ought to teach others, need to be themselves taught the first principles of the oracles of God." No less mournful utterances come up from the bosom of dissent. Hear its voice of lament.

"The dissenting interest is not like itself. I hardly know it. It used to be famous for faith, holiness, and love. I knew the time when I had no doubt, into whatever place of worship I went among dissenters, but that my heart would be warmed and edified, and my edification promoted. Now I hear prayers and sermons which I neither relish nor understand. Evangelical truth and duty are quite old-fashioned things; many pulpits are not so much as chaste; one's ears are so dinned with 'reason,' 'the great law of reason,' and 'the eternal law of reason,' that it is enough to put one out of conceit with the chief excellency of our nature, because it is idolised, and even deified. How prone are men to extremes. O for the purity of our fountains, the wisdom and diligence of our tutors, the humility, piety, and teachableness of our youth."

Such were the voices of those crying like Ishmael in the wilderness, because the fountains were dried up. The causes which had produced so general a decay in vital piety, it hardly falls within our province to describe. We regard it as one of the signs of the times, and descry in it the Lord near at hand, mighty to save. How did the true Israel of God sit solitary, weeping sore in the night. How did the ways of Zion mourn, because none came to her solemn feasts.

Hark! in the distance the heralds cry, "Prepare ye the way of the Lord," and the voice of promise comes richly laden: "Thy light shall break forth as the morning, and thy health shall spring forth speedily. The glory of God shall be thy rereward. Then shalt thou call, and the Lord shall answer; thou shalt cry, and he shall say, Here am I. And if thou draw out thy soul to the hungry, and satisfy the afflicted soul, then shall thy light arise in obscurity, and thy darkness be as the noonday; and the Lord shall guide thee continually, and satisfy thy soul in drought, and make fat thy bones: and thou shalt be like a watered garden, and like a spring of water whose waters fail not. And they that shall be of thee shall build the old waste places: thou shalt raise up the foundations of many generations; and thou shalt be called, The repairer of the breach, The restorer of paths to dwell in."

Thus do the glorious foreshadowings of holy writ adapt themselves to every period of Zion's enlargement: they come forth now to meet and make strong the chosen instruments of this great awakening.

How did the dissenting churches of England receive the new preachers? Did they rejoice and say, "How beautiful upon the mountains are the feet of him that bringeth good tidings, that publisheth salvation?" Some stood aloof, caring for none of these things; others spoke bitterly. Others asked, "Whereunto will this grow?" Others laid all to the charge of enthusiasm, and thought themselves doing God service. "I cannot but think," saith Doddridge, "that by the success of some of these despised men, God is rebuking the madness of those who think themselves the only wise men, and in a remarkable manner laying bare his mighty arm." "There may indeed be, and often is, a tincture of enthusiasm in some extraordinary conversions; but having weighed the matter diligently, I think a man had better be a sober, honest, chaste, industrious enthusiast, than live without any regard to God and religion at all. I think it infinitely better for a man to be a religious Methodist, than an adulterer, a thief, a swearer, a drunkard, or a rebel to his parents, as I knew some actually were who have been wrought upon and reformed by these preachers."

Doddridge was severely censured by his brethren for his ready recognition of Whitefield and Wesley, as true reapers in the Lord's harvest. Angry and threatening letters were sent to him from various quarters, and fears were entertained lest his catholicity might prove ruinous to the institution under his charge; for he not only grasped them by the hand and bade them God speed on their glorious mission, but on coming to London he appeared in their pulpits.

"I am sorry to have had many questions asked me about your preaching in the Tabernacle," wrote Dr Watts anxiously, yet tenderly, "and sinking the character of a clergyman, and especially a tutor among the dissenters, so low thereby. I find many of our friends entertain this idea; but I give no answer, not knowing how much you may have been engaged there. I pray God to guard us from every temptation."

Not long afterwards, Lady Huntingdon, Lady Frances Gardiner, Doddridge, and Mr Price were dining with Lady Abney. The conversation naturally turned upon the remarkable religious movements of the day, when they were candidly discussed, and all, from their separate points of observation, related what their eyes had seen and their ears had heard.

"Such are the fruits," exclaimed the doctor, his small grey eyes brightening with the intensity of his interest, "that will ever follow the faithful proclamation of divine mercy. The Lord our God will crown his message with success, and give it an abundant entrance into the hearts of men. It is a blessing that such men have been raised up." Doddridge probably did not receive another reproof. Dr Watts afterwards became acquainted with Whitefield, who received his almost dying benediction, having paid him a visit a few hours before his death in 1749.

"The nation hath been much alarmed of late with reports concerning the growth and increase of Methodism," said one of the Church of England. "Would we put a stop to the further progress of it? There is one way by which it may be done, and let us of the established church join heart and hand in the work, namely, to live more holily, pray more fervently, preach more heavenly, and labour more diligently than the Methodist ministers appear to do. Then shall we soon hear that field-preaching is at an end, and people will flock to the churches to hear us, as they now flock to the fields to hear them."

To this Doddridge heartily responded, "And let us of the dissenting churches go and do likewise." His earnest prayer was for greater union and harmony among Protestant Christians. "O for that happy time," sighed this healer of breaches, "when the question shall be, not how much we may lawfully dispute, but on the one side, what may we *waive,* and on the other, what may we *acquiesce in,* from a principle of mutual tenderness and respect, without displeasing our common Lord, and injuring that great cause of original Christianity which he hath appointed us to guard. But," he adds, "the darkness of our minds, the narrowness of our hearts, and our attachment to private interest, will put the day, I fear, afar off."

A hundred years later, and we descry not yet its dawn.

3
Doing and Suffering

LADY HUNTINGDON took a warm and active interest in promoting the Redeemer's kingdom; she not only lent her money and her name, but she gave *herself* in personal efforts to seek and to save them which were lost. "For a fortnight past," she writes to Charles Wesley, "I have found that instruction, and some short exhortations to the weak, have been of great use, especially among my work people, with whom I spend a part of every day. I find much comfort in this myself, and am rarely if ever out of the presence of God. He is a pillar of light before me."

Always intent upon seizing opportunities for speaking to her dependents, she once addressed a labourer at work on the garden wall, pressing him with affectionate earnestness to consider eternal things. Some time after, speaking to another upon the same subject, she said, "Thomas, I fear you never pray, or look to Christ for salvation."

"Your ladyship is mistaken," replied the man; "I heard what passed between you and James at the garden wall, and the word you meant for him took effect on me."

"How did you hear it?" she asked.

"I heard it," Thomas answered, "on the other side of the garden, through a hole in the wall, and I shall never forget the impression I received."

In this one little incident we mark the germ of that which constituted the main element of that spiritual awakening – CONQUEST, and conquest in the true line of Christian aggression. An unfledged hope, the quiet possession of spiritual immunities, a merely christened profession, did not satisfy her. She must not only be fed with the bread of life, but she must also feed others; she must not sit down herself at the Master's table, but go out and compel others to come in. At all times and everywhere, men were to be rescued from sin and its terrible penalties; in all the glare, the activity, the interlaced and interlacing interests of the present and outward life, only two things concerned her – redemption, and retribution; they stood out bald and significant, charged with immortal issues: and all her purposes, all her inducements were shaped and carried forward under the urgency of motives as grand and solemn as eternity itself. The folding of the hands, a sweet retirement into unworldly places, a graceful withdrawal from forbidden things, was not *her* testimony to the exceeding sinfulness of sin. She went from the altar and the mercy-seat warmed with holy zeal; her presence aroused the moral consciousness of the most dormant; her whole life was a constant exhortation, "Turn ye, turn ye; for why will ye die?"

In 1744, the earl's family was afflicted by the loss of two beautiful boys, George and Fernando, who died of small-pox, then prevailing at London. With domestic sorrow then mingled public anxiety, the whole country being agitated by the last desperate effort of the exiled Stuarts to regain the throne of England. The nation was filled with alarms and rumours. In many of the larger towns riots occurred, in which the Methodist preachers were sometimes rudely attacked and grossly insulted.

On one occasion Charles Wesley was summoned before the magistrates of Wakefield to answer for treasonable words let fall in prayer, wherein he besought the Lord to recall his "banished" ones, which was construed to mean the Pretender.

"I had no thought of the Pretender," said the accused to the official, "but of those who confess themselves strangers and pilgrims on the earth, who seek a country, knowing this is not their home. The Scripture speaks of us as captive exiles, who are not at home until we reach heaven." The judges wisely accepted the spiritual interpretation, and let the prisoner go.

In the struggle which followed, Colonel Gardiner lost his life. On parting with his wife and eldest daughter at Stirling castle, previous to the fatal engagement at Prestonpans, Lady Frances was more than ordinarily affected: instead of offering his accustomed consolations, and inspiring hope by his own cheerfulness, he only said, "We have an eternity to spend together."

The fall of this excellent man not only bereaved a large and fond family, but spread sorrow over a wide circle of friends, and sadness through the nation. Heavy are the costs of war – "and heavy is this affliction to Lady Frances and the children," exclaimed Lady Huntingdon; "but he has gone to the great Captain of his salvation, to sing the wonders of that love which hath redeemed him, and made him meet for the saints in light." So does "hope in Christ" point heavenward. Doddridge preached an impressive sermon upon the occasion, which was afterwards published, and a hundred copies sent to Lady Huntingdon for circulation. At a later date appeared his well-known memoir, which has been read and re-read all over the world.

Within less than a year, Lady Frances Gardiner was called to reciprocate the sympathies of her friend. Earl Huntingdon died of apoplexy on the 13th of October, 1746, at his mansion in Downing Street, Westminster, aged fifty, leaving his wife at the age of thirty-nine in the sole charge of his family and fortune. He was a man of unblemished character, and though not a believer in the distinctive theology of his wife, he courteously entertained her religious friends, and listened with admiration to the eloquent preachers of that day. "The morality of the Bible I admire," he says, "but the doctrine of the atonement I cannot understand."

His sisters were eminent for their piety, and Margaret became the wife of Rev Benjamin Ingham, whose preaching first led her to the Saviour. After the earl's death, the family retired to Donnington Park, where the countess spent in privacy the first six months of her widowhood. Some extracts from her letters to Doddridge admit us to the inner sanctuary of her heart.

"I hope you will never care about the ceremony of time in your letters to me, but just when attended with greatest ease to yourself, for we both agree that the one thing worth living for must be proclaiming the love of God to man in Christ Jesus. As for me, I want no holiness he does not give me; I can wish for no liberty but what he likes for me, and I am satisfied with every misery he does not redeem me from, that in all things I may feel, 'without him I can do nothing.'

"My family consists of two sons and as many daughters; for all of them I have nothing to do but to praise God. The children of so many prayers and tears, I doubt not shall one day be blest, your prayers for us all helping. The hint you gave me is a great matter of joy to me; my soul longeth for grace. May the Lord give us all such love, to live and to die to him, and for him alone. I am, with most kind respects for Mrs Doddridge, your most sincere, but weak and unworthy friend,

"S. H."

Again she writes, "Some important time is coming. Oh, might I hope it is that time when all things shall be swallowed up by the enlightening and comforting displays of our glorious Redeemer's kingdom. My hopes are not only full of immortality, but of this. Your works are blessed, and God is making you a polished shaft in his quiver. I want everybody to pray with you and for you, that you may wax stronger and stronger. I have had a letter from Lord Bolingbroke, who says, 'I desire my compliments and thanks to Dr Doddridge, and I hope I shall continue to deserve his good opinion.'"

During the lifetime of the earl, Lady Huntingdon's time was necessarily engrossed by many cares, which withheld her from the friends and the interests which lay nearest to her heart. As mistress of his princely mansions, she had duties to general society which could not be slighted; respect and affection for him controlled her private preferences, and without making her disloyal to her religious convictions, blended her interests with his own. The tie is now broken: she meekly bears the chastisement; more than ever she feels herself a stranger and a pilgrim in the present and outward world; more than ever she feels herself a subject of that spiritual kingdom which Christ came to set up; and henceforth we find unfolding that lofty energy of character, which has identified her name with the revived Christianity of her day.

Returning again to society, Lady Huntingdon may be seen journeying through Wales. The party is large, composed of her two daughters, her sisters Anne and Frances Hastings, several clergymen, and other religious friends. Is it a jaunt of pleasure? A tour of aimless excitement? A seeing of new things for the sake of killing time?

Let us first pause and look around on the moral wastes of this English soil. "While there was little zeal in the great body of the clergy," says Southey, "many causes combined which rendered this want of zeal more and more injurious. The population had doubled since the settlement of the church under Elizabeth, yet no provision had been made for increasing proportionally the means of moral and religious instruction, which in the beginning had been insufficient. In reality, though the temporal advantages of Christianity extended to all classes, the great majority of the populace knew nothing more of religion than its forms. They had been Papists formerly, and now were Protestants, but they had never been Christians. The Reformation had taken away the ceremonies to which they were attached, and substituted nothing in their stead. There was the Bible indeed, but to the great body of the labouring people, the Bible was, even in the letter, a sealed book."

Here then was the rudeness of the peasantry, the brutality of the town populace, the prevalence of drunkenness, the growth of impiety, a general deadness to religion; and it was this brutish ignorance, this stiff-necked degradation, this famine of the Word of God and all means of moral elevation, which at once demanded the labours of such men as Whitefield, Wesley, and their coadjutors, and inspired them with that resistless zeal which made their preaching like the fire and the hammer upon the flinty rock. Everywhere, on all sides, was *spiritual want;* it was not only seen among the abandoned, but felt in the general indifference to religion among the middling classes, in the sceptical spirit which pervaded the higher, and the almost total lack of earnestness in professed Christians, both among the clergy and laity.

What a demand for labourers on this harvest-field! The single and uppermost thought of those raised up of God and sent to these famishing multitudes was, "To the rescue!" Their simple and heartfelt message was, "Repent, and believe on the Lord Jesus Christ." This was not only the pervading element of the preachers, but also of private Christians. As Christ came to seek and to save them which were lost, so must his disciples go forth bearing his invitations of mercy, leading men from sin and shame to those ways which are pleasantness, and for those paths which are peace.

So felt Lady Huntingdon. The party set out from Bath, and in its journey through Wales travelled slowly, stopping at the towns and villages on the route, in order to give the preachers an opportunity of addressing the people whenever a congregation could be gathered. Multitudes flocked to hear them.

Indeed, the preachers knew something of their hearers: one of them was *Griffith Jones* of Abercowyn, author of a plan for instructing his countrymen, known as the "Welsh circulating schools." The ignorance and heathenism of the peasantry he had deeply deplored. On his first settlement in 1711, before he admitted communicants, he began by carefully examining them in Christian doctrine; but he soon found that those who most needed the instruction, men grown up in ignorance, were unwilling to attend, because unable to answer the questions put to them. He then fixed upon Saturday before the communion for distributing to the poor their supply of bread, bought with the money collected at the previous communion. These he gathered into a class, and by his great kindness of manner won their confidence and love, until he at last encouraged them to learn short lessons from the Bible. Thus it became a custom among his poor parishioners to repeat a verse of Scripture on receiving their monthly allowance of bread. By this direct and personal intercourse with the poor, he learned how vague and imperfect were their notions of Christianity, and how little the Sabbath service could effect, without the aid of other means of instruction. With this data he resolved to act, and his first school was established in 1730 in one of his parishes, Llanddowror. Another soon followed; and these were attended with results so obviously good, that he soon received the cooperation of several efficient persons, and a generous donation of Bibles and other books from the Society for Promoting Christian Knowledge.

In ten years, one hundred and twenty-eight schools were in operation, with nearly eight thousand persons taught to read the Scriptures in the Welsh language, catechised, instructed in psalmody, and under the general supervision of Christian schoolmasters, trying in various ways to promote their best good. Griffith Jones was a popular as well as a faithful preacher; his greatest excellence was "gavaelgar ar y gydwybod," or a *grasp on the conscience;* and accustomed as he had been to preaching-tours, and grey as he had grown in the service of his hardy countrymen, his very presence was like the ringing of the Sabbath bells for the people to come and hear.

Beside him is a younger brother, a Welsh Boanerges, *Howell Harris.* Greet him and cherish him, for he deserves well of those who love the Lord. Though destined for the church, he received no serious impressions until twenty-one, when this passage from a sermon, "If you are unfit to visit the table of the Lord, you are unfit to visit the church, you are unfit to live and unfit to die," fastened powerfully upon his conscience. On his way from church, meeting a person whom he had wronged, he instantly confessed his fault and begged to be forgiven; and though fears and remorse for a long time darkened his soul, he stoutly determined to give himself to the service of God, and began to warn his neighbours to flee from the wrath to come. In 1735 he returned to Oxford to complete his studies, but the immoralities of the university disgusted him, and he returned home. He betook himself henceforth to the poor of his native land. In the cottage and the field he is preaching the doctrines of the cross. So many came to him for instruction, that at the close of the year he formed them into societies. "In the formation of these," he tells us, "I followed the rules of Dr Woodward, in a book written by him on the subject. Previously to this, no societies of the kind had been founded either in England or Wales. The English Methodists had not become famous as yet, although, as I afterwards learned, several of them in Oxford were at that time under strong religious influences."

They were not organised either as Methodist or dissenting congregations, nor indeed with any view of their ever separating from the church. The revival of religion in the church was his avowed purpose at first, and his proposed object through life.

In 1739 Whitefield and Harris met for the first time in the town-hall of Cardiff, where the former, fresh from the glowing scenes of Bristol, poured forth his impassioned eloquence to his Welsh auditory, among whom was Howell Harris. Of the mutual delight afforded by the interview, which immediately afterwards took place, Whitefield said characteristically, "I doubt not that Satan envied our happiness; but I hope by the help of God we shall make his kingdom shake."

Such then were the men attached to Lady Huntingdon's party. On arriving at Trevecca, Brecknockshire, the birthplace of Howell Harris, they remained several days, the preachers addressing, four or five times a day, immense crowds, who came from all the country round about. Twenty years afterwards, Trevecca was one of the principal centres of the countess' influence.

"On a review of all that I have seen and heard," exclaimed she, on their return home, "I am constrained to cry, 'Bless the Lord, O my soul, and all that is within me bless his holy name.' The sermons contained the most solemn and awful truths, such as the utter ruin of man by the fall and his redemption by the Lord Jesus Christ, the energetic declaration of which produced quite a sensible effect on many, who, there is reason to believe, were brought from nature's darkness to the marvellous light of the all-glorious gospel. My earnest prayer to God for them is, that they may continue in his grace and truth."

Of a journey thus conducted, we cannot but regret that the only memorials are the brief sketches of a hastily penned journal by Lady Frances Hastings. Though undertaken for the countess' health, it seems really to have been a home missionary tour; a rare union, we may venture to assert, in those days as well as our own, when travelling, even among professing Christians, is too often a time for "casting off fear and restraining prayer."

Not long after the countess' return, Doddridge paid a visit to London. During his stay he thus writes to his wife: "I can conclude by telling you that I am at the close of one of the most pleasant days I shall ever spend without you. After an hour's charming conversation with Lady Huntingdon and Mrs Edwin, I preached in her family by express desire, and met Colonel Gumley, who is really a second Colonel Gardiner. After dinner the ladies entertained us with their voices and a harpsichord, with which I was highly delighted; and I have stolen a hymn which I believe to have been written by good Lady Huntingdon, and which I shall not fail to communicate to you. She is quite a mother to the poor; she visits them and prays with them in sickness, and they leave their children to her for a legacy when they die, and she takes care of them. I was really astonished at the traces of religion which I discovered in her and Mrs Edwin, and cannot but glorify God for them. More cheerfulness I never saw mingled with so much devotion. Lady Frances Gardiner sets out on Monday next. I have taken my leave of her."

4
Whitefield

IN 1728 there was a young man struggling through Oxford, paying his way as servitor at Pembroke college. "At first he was rendered uncomfortable by the society into which he was thrown: he had several chamber-fellows, who would fain have made him join in their riotous mode of life; and as he could only escape from their persecutions by sitting alone in his study, he was sometimes benumbed with cold; but when they perceived the strength as well as the singularity of his character, they suffered him to take his own way in peace."

Before he came to Oxford, he had heard of the young men there "who lived by rule and method," and were therefore called *Methodists*. They were now much talked of, and generally despised. He, however, was drawn towards them by kindred feelings, defended them strenuously when he heard them reviled, and when he saw them go through a jeering crowd to receive the Lord's Supper at St Mary's, was strongly inclined to follow their example. For more than a year he yearned to be acquainted with them, but it seems that a sense of his inferior condition kept him back. At length the great object of his desires was effected. A pauper had attempted suicide, and he sent a poor woman to inform Charles Wesley, that he might visit the person and administer spiritual medicine; the messenger was charged not to say who sent her; contrary to these orders she told his name, and Charles Wesley, who had seen him frequently walking by himself, and heard something of his character, invited him to breakfast the next morning. An introduction to this little fellowship soon followed, and he also, like them, "began to live by rule, and pick up the very fragments of his time, that not a moment of it might be lost."

This young man was *George Whitefield*, and thus has the graphic pen of Wesley's biographer described his first introduction to that little society, whose members afterwards stamped their influence so broadly on that and subsequent time.

After leaving Oxford and taking deacon's orders, he began to preach at Bristol, and exhibit that impassioned eloquence which moved and melted both the Old World and the New. He preached about five times a week to such congregations that it was with great difficulty that he could make his way along the crowded aisles to the reading-desk. "Some hung upon the rails of the organ-loft, others climbed upon the leads of the church, and all together made the church so hot with their breath, that the steam would fall from the pillars like drops of rain." When he preached his farewell-sermon, and said to the people that perhaps they might see his face no more, high and low, old and young, burst into tears. Multitudes, after the sermon, followed him home weeping; the next day he was employed from seven in the morning until midnight in talking and giving spiritual advice to awakened hearers; and he left Bristol secretly in the middle of the night, to avoid the ceremony of being escorted by horsemen and coaches out of the town.

While at London it was necessary to place constables at the doors, both within and without, such multitudes assembled; and on Sunday mornings in the latter months of the year, long before day, you might have seen the streets filled with people going to hear him, with lanterns in their hands.

"The man who produced such extraordinary effects," says Southey, "had many natural advantages. He was something above the middle stature, well proportioned, though at this time slender, and remarkable for a native gracefulness of manner. His complexion was very fair, his eyes small and lively, of a dark blue colour; in recovering from the measles, he had contracted a squint with one of them, but this peculiarity rather rendered the expression of his countenance more remarkable, than in any degree lessened the effect of its uncommon sweetness. His voice excelled both in melody and compass, and its fine modulations were happily accompanied by that grace of action which he possessed in an eminent degree, and which has been said to be the chief requisite of an orator." Garrick said he could make men weep or tremble at his varied utterance of the word *Mesopotamia*.

To these natural gifts and graces was added a deep conviction of the greatness and the grandeur of his calling, as a messenger of God. His maxim was to preach as Apelles painted, for *eternity.* When, a young man, Dr Delany once remarked in his hearing, "I wish, whenever I go into the pulpit, to look upon it as the last time that I may ever preach, or the last time the people may hear." This, Whitefield never forgot. He often said, "Would ministers preach for eternity, they would act the part of true Christian orators, for then they would endeavour to move the affections and warm the heart, and not constrain their hearers to suspect that they dealt in the false commerce of unfelt truth."

Whitefield broke away from the popularity thus strongly flowing in upon him, to follow his beloved college companions the Wesleys to the New World; but not, as he expected, to labour with them in Georgia, for the ship which carried him sailed from the Downs only a few hours before that which brought Wesley home anchored on the English coast.

He remained a year in Georgia, where he seems not to have experienced any of those peculiar trials which hindered the usefulness of Wesley. He returned to England in 1739, in order to receive deacon's orders and to raise contributions for the establishment of an orphan-house at Bethesda, twelve miles from Savannah, after the famous model of Professor Franke's in Halle; the history and success of which seems to have created a profound interest among the Christians of that day, when charitable institutions of any magnitude scarcely existed, and long before the great religious associations of our time had been conceived.

Among the news of this period, the celebrated Countess of Hereford thus writes to a friend on the continent: "I do not know whether you have heard of a new sect, who call themselves Methodists. There is one Whitefield at the head of them, a young man of five and twenty, who has for some months gone about preaching in the fields and market-places in the country, and in London at Mayfair and Moorfields, to ten or twelve thousand people at a time. He went to Georgia with General Oglethorpe, and returned to take priest's orders, which he did; and I believe since that time hardly a day has passed that he has not preached once, and generally twice. At first, he and some of his brethren seemed only to aim at restoring the practice of the primitive Christians as to daily sacraments, stated fasts, frequent prayers, relieving prisoners, visiting the sick, and giving alms to the poor; but upon sound men refusing these men their pulpits, they have betaken themselves to preaching in the fields, and they have such crowds of followers, that they have set in a flame all the clergy in the kingdom, who represent them as hypocrites and enthusiasts. As to the latter epithet, some passages in Mr Whitefield's latest journals seem to countenance the accusation; but I think their manner of living has not afforded any grounds to suspect them of hypocrisy. The Bishop of London, however, has thought it necessary to write a pastoral letter to warn the people of his diocese against being led away by them; and Dr Trapp has published a sermon upon 'the great folly and danger of being righteous overmuch,' a doctrine which does not seem absolutely necessary to be preached to the people of the present age."

It was not until his second visit to America and return to England, that a difference of theological views began to cloud the friendship which had subsisted between the two distinguished preachers, Whitefield and John Wesley. We should approach the rupture with sadness, only as such things "must needs be" in our present state of imperfect knowledge and feeble grace.

While the storm was brewing, "My honoured friend and brother," wrote Whitefield to Wesley, "for once hearken to a child, who is willing to wash your feet. I beseech you, by the mercies of God in Christ Jesus our Lord, if you would have my love confirmed towards you, write no more to me about the misrepresentations wherein we differ. Why should we dispute, when there is no possibility of convincing? Will it not in the end destroy brotherly love, and insensibly take from us that cordial union and sweetness of soul, which I pray God may always subsist between us? How glad would the enemies of the Lord be to see us divided. How would the cause of our common Master every way suffer by our raising disputes about particular points of doctrine. Honoured sir, let us offer salvation freely to all by the blood of Jesus, and whatever light God has communicated to us, let us freely communicate to others."

Happy were it for the Christian world, if the admirable temper of this letter could govern its divided friends and clashing sects; but admirable as it was, and however it might have conciliated the resolute and uncompromising spirit of Wesley, the breach widened, for on both sides there were friends and followers who fanned the flame, and Whitefield afterwards wrote in an altered and recriminating tone.

With such questions at issue, involving points of doctrine which no human intellect has ever mastered, a rupture became inevitable. When Whitefield returned to the scene of his early triumphs, "he came to his own, and his own received him not." His Kingswood school was in the hands of Wesley; and at London a temporary shed, called the Tabernacle, served to shelter his spiritual children since their exodus from the foundry.

At this period Whitefield says sadly, "The world is angry with me, and numbers of my own spiritual children. Some say, that God will destroy me in a fortnight, and that my fall will be as great as Peter's. Scarce one comes to see me from morning till night, and on Kennington Common I have not above a hundred to hear me. I am much embarrassed in my circumstances. A thousand pounds I owe for the orphan-house. I am threatened to be arrested for two hundred pounds more. My travelling expenses also are to be defrayed. A family of one hundred to be daily maintained, four thousand miles off, in the dearest place of the king's dominions – all my work is to *begin* again."

Their counsels divided and their ranks broken, there *seemed* to be a weak betrayal of their Master's cause. Were the Apolloses and Cephases thus to come in and assert their shallow claims, and plunder the church of her men and means? It was not so to be.

In spite of the dissents and jarrings which must needs come, the leaders of that day more truly comprehended their mission; their spiritual gains were not to be scattered, nor their spiritual strength wasted in a bitter household squabble: there was a worthier work for them. Whitefield and Wesley loved each other, and the soul of each glowed with the warm charities of the gospel; they loved a common Master, whose cause lay nearest their hearts, and while each proclaimed its great normal principle, *salvation by a crucified Redeemer,* with a loving earnestness, each linked with it his own peculiar system of doctrines.

When we see the chafing and champing of worldly and sometimes even religious men at the ebbing of their popularity, it is encouraging to turn to one who not only knew the solidity of his own principles, but could steadily anchor on them and calmly take the surges and the spray.

"What is a little scourge of the tongue?" says Whitefield. "What is a thrusting out of the synagogue? The time of temptation will be, when we are thrust into an inner prison and feel the iron entering into our souls, God's people may be permitted to forsake us for a while, but the Lord Jesus can stand by us. And if thou, dearest Redeemer, wilt strengthen me in my inward man, let enemies plunge me into a fiery furnace, or throw me into a den of lions. Let us suffer for Jesus with a cheerful heart. His love will sweeten every cup, though never so bitter. May all disputing soon cease, and each of us talk of *nothing but Him crucified: this is my resolution.*"

And his life corresponded to it, in adversity as well as in prosperity. Herein was the singleness of Whitefield's piety: one aim governed and sustained him through a long and laborious career – and it was *preaching Christ.*

At what time Lady Huntingdon first became acquainted with Whitefield does not appear. On her return from Wales, he was expected in England from his third visit to America. When he landed at Deal, she immediately sent Howell Harris to bring him to her own house in Chelsea, where he preached to large circles of the showy world, who thronged this fashionable watering-place. For the benefit of this class of hearers, she soon after removed to London, appointed Whitefield her chaplain, and during the winter of 1748-49 opened her splendid mansion in Park Street for the ministrations of the gospel.

"Good Lady Huntingdon," writes he, "has come to town, and I am to preach twice a week at her house to the great and noble. O that some of them might be effectually called to taste the riches of redeeming love." On the day appointed, Chesterfield, Bolingbroke, and a circle of the nobility attended; and having heard him once, they desired to come again. "Lord Chesterfield thanked me," he says. "Lord Bolingbroke was moved, and asked me to come and see him the next morning. My hands have been full of work, and I have been among great company. All accepted my sermons. Thus the world turns round: '*In all time of my wealth, good Lord, deliver me.*'"

Although Whitefield used the current compliments of address common to that period, more fulsome then than now in England, and at either time sounding oddly enough to us in the United States of America, he never betrayed his office as the minister of God, but warned, rebuked, and exhorted men with all fidelity, as well as with all affection.

"As for *praying in your family*, I entreat you not to neglect it," he said to the old Scottish Marquis of Lothian, who would fain have been like Nicodemus, a Christian in the dark. "You are bound to do it. Apply to Christ to overcome your present fears; they are the effects of pride or infidelity, or both."

The death-bed of Lord St John, who was one of the hearers of this parlour preaching, exhibited scenes unusual in the circle where he moved: the Bible was read to him, and his cry was, "God be merciful to me a sinner!" "My Lord Bolingbroke," wrote Lady Huntingdon to Whitefield, "was much struck with his brother's language in his last moments. O that his eyes might be opened by the illuminating influence of divine truth. He is a singularly awful character; and I am fearfully alarmed, lest the gospel which he so heartily despises, yet affects to reverence, should prove the savour of death unto death to him.

"Some, I trust, are savingly awakened, while many are inquiring; thus the great Lord of the harvest hath put honour on your ministry, and hath given my heart an encouraging token of the utility of our feeble efforts."

Under her auspices, a prayer-meeting was established for those females who, from the circles of rank and fashion, became the followers of the Lord.

Among these were Lady Frances Gardiner, Lady Mary Hamilton, daughter of the Marquis of Lothian, who had attended the ministry of Whitefield in Scotland, Lady Gertrude Hotham and Countess Delitz, sisters of Lady Chesterfield, Lady Chesterfield herself, and Lady Fanny Shirley, of whom Horace Walpole wrote in his scoffing way to a friend on the continent, "If you ever think of returning to England, you must prepare yourself with Methodism: this sect increases as fast as ever almost any other religious nonsense did. Lady Fanny Shirley has chosen this way of bestowing the dregs of her beauty, and Mr Lyttleton is very near making the same sacrifice of the dregs of all those various characters that he has worn. The Methodists love your big sinners, and indeed they have a plentiful harvest."

"There needed," said one, "strong consolation in order to resist the strong temptations presented by a frivolous court, a witty peerage, and a learned bench in favour of a formal religion. Nothing but the 'joy of the Lord' could have sustained them in such a sphere. Happiness in religion was the best security for their holiness. They could not be laughed out of a good hope through grace. Wit or banter may make persisting a weakness or a fancy, but they cannot make hope, peace, and joy appear absurd. Neither the severe denunciations of Warburton, nor the polished sarcasm of Chesterfield, could touch the consciousness of peace in believing, or of enjoyment in secret prayer, in the hearts of those ladies who had found at the cross and the mercy-seat the happiness they had sought in vain from the world."

"Religion was never so much the subject of conversation as now," writes Lady Huntingdon to Doddridge. "Some of the great ones hear with me the gospel patiently, and thus much seed is sown by Mr Whitefield's preaching. O that it may fall on good ground, and bring forth abundantly.

"I had the pleasure, yesterday, of Mr Gibbon's and Mr Crittenden's company to dine with me. Lord Lothian and Lady Frances Gardiner gave them the meeting, and we had truly a most primitive and heavenly day; our hearts and voices praised the Lord, prayed to him, and talked of him. I had another lady present, whose face, since I saw you last, is turned Zion-ward. Of the 'honourable women,' I trust there are not a few; patience shall have its proper work: and if we love our Lord, we must be tender over his lambs. I trust He will assist us to keep fanning the flame in every heart; this, my friend, is our joyful task for the best Master we can serve, for time or eternity. Do not let our hands hang down; we must wrestle for ourselves and for all dead in their sins, till the day break and the shadows of time flee away."

While thus solicitous for the spiritual welfare of those of her own rank, no less interested is she in her humbler neighbours; to them her house was constantly opened, that they also might be enriched by "that faith which comes by hearing." On week-days her kitchen was filled by the poor of the flock, whom she supplied with all the means of religious profit which lay in her power.

Meanwhile good and evil tidings come from Wales. The winter campaign of Howell Harris is attended with stormy weather. The gentry frown, the magistrates bristle, while the poor people, who hunger for His "good words," are sorely oppressed, nay, grievously tormented. On one excursion he did not take off his clothes for seven days and nights, being obliged to meet his little congregation in solitary places at midnight, or by daylight in ravine or cleft, in order to avoid the persecuting vigilance of their enemies. "One man," says Harris, "was obliged to pay Sir Watkins Wynn twenty shillings, several of my poor hearers five shillings, and one who paid the same sum before, was fined seven shillings more; and this is the third time my poor sheep of this fold have been thus served."

When the matter came to Lady Huntingdon's knowledge, indignant at the injustice and bigotry of Sir Watkins Wynn, with characteristic energy she instantly made a representation to the government of his infringement of the Act of Toleration; the magistrates were rebuked by the higher law, and Sir Watkins was ordered to return the fines to the pockets of the sufferers.

Honourable exceptions, however, were there among the Welsh magistrates. Harris having made an appointment to meet the peasantry near Garth, in Breconshire, the residence of Sir Marmaduke Gwynne, that gentleman, frightened by the reports concerning him, resolved on the occasion to do his duty as a magistrate, and stop proceedings of so disorderly and mobbish a character. Regarding the missionary as neither more nor less than a firebrand to church and state, Mr Magistrate Gwynne prepared for a resolute attack, but wisely enough said to his family on going out, "I'll first *hear* the man myself, before I commit him." Accordingly he mingled with the congregation, lying in wait to pounce upon the preacher at every next word. "Why, he's neither more nor less than an apostle," cried Gwynne inwardly, his stout heart melting under the manner and earnest language of the man of God. The Riot Act lay asleep in his pocket, and at the end of the discourse he marched up to the rude platform, shook the preacher warmly by the hand, confessed his intention, asked his pardon, bade him preach while he lived, and took him back to Garth to supper. Henceforth the countenance of the Gwynne family smiled on the new movements. Regardless of public or private censure, Sir Marmaduke stood stoutly up for the evangelists, and used all his influence for promoting the spread of the gospel in the regions round about. One of his daughters afterwards married Charles Wesley.

In February, 1749, Whitefield left London a short time to recruit amid scenes less exciting, for *rest* he never knew. Lady Huntingdon goes to Clifton. Her eldest son has become of age, and as Earl Huntingdon, takes possession of Donnington Park, Ledstone Hall, with other patrimony belonging to his title. He then set out upon the fashionable continental tour. At Paris he is warmly greeted by the most distinguished English residents, particularly introduced as he is by Lord Chesterfield, who pronounces him "one of the first peers of England, with merit and talents equal to his birth."

Lady Elizabeth Hastings, the countess' eldest daughter, much admired for her grace, vivacity, and abilities, in March of this year was appointed "Lady of the Bedchamber" to the princesses Amelia and Caroline, sisters of George III. She remained in office but a few months. In relation to it, Horace Walpole said, "The queen of the Methodists got her daughter named for Lady of the Bedchamber to the princesses; but it is all off again, as she will not let her play cards on Sunday."

5

Romaine – Alarms

HERE comes one with quick, elastic step; his eye is keen; his thin, yet strongly lined face is surmounted by a grey wig somewhat smitten by the hand of time; his plain, and certainly not polished manners, are perhaps in keeping with the blue suit and coarse blue yarn stockings, in which he is usually seen; he cannot stop for all the elaborate courtesies of life, for manifold cares and duties eat up his time, which he is bent on using wisely, as one who must give account. Behold *Rev William Romaine*, curate of St Dunstan's and St George's, Hanover Square, London, whose searching and pungent appeals were at once the scorn and the delight of multitudes, and whose "*Walk of Faith*" held a prominent place on the bookshelves of our fathers fifty years ago.

He was at Oxford with Whitefield and the Wesleys, whom on account of their religious strictness and singularity he then avoided and despised. Whatever might have been his literary hopes or ambitious longings, he was the child of prayer, and trained by believing parents for the service of God. Thoroughly instructed in the doctrines of the cross, he at length cordially embraced them, and the unfeigned faith which dwelt in his parents now became a living principle within his own bosom.

Having taken orders, he occasionally preached, but for seven years his time had been chiefly occupied in preparing for the press a new edition of the Hebrew Concordance and Lexicon of Marius de Calasio; and it was to further its progress with the printers that we find him in London in 1747, then thirty-three years of age. Having completed his arrangements, he determined to return to the north of England, where his friends resided, and where he was best known. His trunk was on shipboard, and he was hurriedly threading his way through the bustle of Cheapside on his route to the quay, when a stranger suddenly stopped him and asked if his name were not Romaine. "That is my name," answered the astonished young man. "I knew your father, and I saw at a glance the father's look in the son," continued the gentleman. The two stood and talked. Before parting the stranger spoke of his interest in the vacant parishes of St George and St Botolph, and offered to exert it on his behalf; and thus, on this chance and abrupt meeting, did the young preacher pause and make choice of his destiny for life.

"Had not Mr Romaine met this stranger – had not the stranger been instantly struck with the son's resemblance to his father – had he not accosted him with a curiosity for which probably he himself could give no reason – had he passed a moment sooner or later – had the lectureship not been vacant – had not the conversation led to the cause of Mr Romaine's leaving – in short," says Dr Haweis, "if a thousand unforeseen circumstances had not concurred just at that critical moment, the labours of that great reviver of evangelical truth in the churches of London, humanly speaking, had been lost to the metropolis, and with it all the blessed consequences of his ministry, which thousands have experienced, and for which they will bless God to all eternity. Thus doeth He who holds the thread of every circumstance: we are the web of his own great purposes.

A general alarm prevailed in London at this time, 1749, for fear of coming judgments. The universal corruption of morals, the mocking spirit of irreligion, and the heartlessness and hollowness of society on one side, the bold rebukes, the searching appeals, the fearless denunciations of the new preachers on the other, united with the report of earthquakes desolating and destroying on the continent, conspired to kindle in the public mind a consciousness of deserved wrath, and a fearful apprehension of approaching calamities. There are times when whole communities are thus startled into a sense of God, and great fears lay hold upon them. The shocks of earthquake were now more sensibly felt in London than for many years. Houses were shaken, chimneys were thrown down, multitudes left the city, while crowds fled for safety to the open fields. Tower Hill, Kennington Common, and Moorfields were thronged with men, women, and children. Places of worship became crowded. The Wesleys preached incessantly, and Whitefield went out one time at midnight to address a dismayed and affrighted multitude in Hyde Park. Romaine also was intent upon improving these solemn opportunities.

In addition to his forcible appeals from the pulpit, and his faithful conversations in private, he published *"An Alarm to the Careless World,"* which might speak where his voice could never reach. A sermon also appeared from the pen of Dr Doddridge, entitled, *"The Guilt and Doom of Capernaum seriously recommended to the Inhabitants of London."*

"You have now, sirs," he says in the preface, "very lately had repeated and surprising demonstrations of the almighty power of that infinite and adorable Being, whom in the midst of your hurries and amusements you are so ready to forget. His hand hath once and again, within these five weeks, lifted up your mighty city from its basis, and shook its million inhabitants in their dwellings. The palaces of the great, nay, even of the greatest, have not been exempted, that the princes of the land might be wise, and its judges and lawgivers might receive instruction. And is not the voice of this earthquake like that of the angel in the Apocalypse, flying in the midst of heaven, and having the everlasting gospel, saying with a loud voice, 'Fear God, and give glory to him, and worship him that made heaven and earth'?

"I suppose what you have so lately felt, to be the result of natural causes; but remember, they were causes disposed by Him who, from the day in which he founded our island and laid the foundations of the earth, knew every circumstance of their operation with infinitely more certainty than the most skilful engineer the disposition and success of a mine which he hath prepared and directed, and which he fires in the appointed moment. And do not your hearts meditate terror? Especially when you consider how much London hath done, and even you yourselves have done, to provoke the eyes of his holiness and awaken the vengeance of his almighty arm? The second shock, it seems, was more dreadful than the first; and may not the third be yet more dreadful than the second? So that this last may seem as a merciful signal to prepare for what may with the most terrible propriety be called an untimely grave indeed – a grave that shall receive the living with the dead. Think what you have lately felt; and think whether in that amazing moment you could have done anything material to prepare for another world, if eternity had depended upon that momentary preparation. A shriek of wild consternation, a cry as you were sinking, 'The Lord have mercy on us!' would probably have been of very little significancy to those that have so long despised mercy, and would not have thought of asking it but in the last extremity."

"Oh London, London," cries the preacher later in his sermon, "dear city of my birth and education, seat of so many of my friends, seat of our princes and senators, centre of our commune, heart of our island which must feel and languish and tremble and die with thee, how art thou lifted up to heaven; how high do thy glories rise, and how bright do they shine! How great is thy magnificence; how extensive thy commerce; how numerous, how free, how happy thine inhabitants; how happy, above all, in their religious opportunities; how happy in the uncorrupted gospel, so long and so faithfully preached in thy synagogues! But while we survey these heights of elevation, must we not tremble lest thou shouldst fall so much the lower, lest thou shouldst plunge so much the deeper in ruin?

"My situation, sirs, is not such as renders me most capable of judging concerning the moral character of this our celebrated metropolis. But who can hear what seem the most credible reports of it, and not take an alarm? Whose spirit must not, like that of Paul at Athens, be stirred, when he sees the city so abandoned to profaneness, luxury, and vanity? Is it indeed false, all that we hear? Is it indeed accidental, all that we see? Is London wronged, when it is said that great licentiousness reigns among most of its inhabitants, and great indolence and indifference to religion, even among those who are not licentious? that assemblies for divine worship are much neglected, or frequented with little appearance of seriousness or solemnity, while assemblies for pleasure are thronged, and attended with such eagerness that all the heart and soul seems to be given to them rather than to God; that the Sabbath, instead of being religiously observed, is given to jaunts of pleasure into neighbouring villages, or wasted on beds of sloth, or at tables of excess; that men of every rank are ambitious of appearing to be something more than they are, grasping at business they cannot manage, entering into engagements they cannot answer, and so, after a vain and contemptible blaze, drawing bankruptcy upon themselves and others? that the poorer sort are grossly ignorant, wretchedly depraved, and abandoned to the most brutal sensualities and infirmities; while those who would exert any remarkable zeal to remedy these evils, by introducing a deep and warm sense of religion into the minds of others, are suspected and censured as whimsical and enthusiastical, if not designing men? in a word, that the religion of our divine Master is by multitudes of the great and the vulgar openly renounced and blasphemed? Men and brethren, are these things indeed so? I take not upon me to answer absolutely that they are: but I will venture to say, that if they are indeed thus, London, as rich and grand and glorious as it is, has reason to tremble, and to tremble so much the more for its abused riches, grandeur, and glory."

While some of the preachers were thus careful to improve the general alarm by a vigorous enforcement of divine truth, there were multitudes of the people no less anxious for spiritual instruction. St George's, where Romaine preached, was thronged; and of this, some of the regular parishioners grievously complained. The old Earl of Northampton reminded them that they bore the greater crowd of a ballroom, an assembly, and a playhouse, without inconvenience or complaint; "and if," said he, "the power to attract be imputed as a matter of admiration to Garrick, why should it be urged as a crime against Romaine? Shall excellence be exceptionable only in divine things?"

But the thing was not to be borne. If the parishioners could bear the preaching of the curate, the rector would not. Zeal in the preacher was at that time looked upon, in certain quarters, as one of the unpardonable sins of the pulpit; for it reflected discredit upon a large body of the clergy, and whether he meant it or not, was a rebuke upon the dead and formal ministry of his brethren. Romaine was therefore summarily dismissed from his curacy. Turned out of St George's, but reluctant to part from many of his parishioners, he ventured to meet them at the house of one of their number; for which alleged irregularity he was threatened with prosecution from the ecclesiastical court. On learning this, Lady Huntingdon immediately invited him to her house in Park Street, offered him her scarf, and made him her chaplain. Thus shielded by a peeress of the realm, he continued his labours, more vigorously than ever, for the spiritual good of his fellows. Romaine was at this time thirty-five years of age.

"God has been terribly shaking the metropolis," wrote Whitefield to Lady Huntingdon. "I hope it is an earnest of his giving a shock to secure sinners, and making them to cry out, 'What shall we do to be saved?' I trust, honoured madam, you have been brought to believe on the Lord Jesus. What a mercy is this: to be plucked as a brand from the burning, to be one of those few *mighty* and *noble* that are called effectually by the grace of God. What can shake a soul whose hopes are fixed on the Rock of ages? Winds may blow, rains may and will descend even upon persons in the most exalted stations, but they that trust in the Lord never shall, never can be totally confounded."

As the season advances, we turn from the exciting scenes of the metropolis, from its din and depravity, to the green lawns and haw-thorn hedges of the country. We hear the lark,

"– *Blithe spirit,*
Pouring its full heart
In profuse strains of unpremeditated art;"

we cross the Ouse, perhaps at Olney, and see "displayed its lilies newly blown;" and following Whitefield, find him at Northampton in the hospitable home of Dr Doddridge. The famous and somewhat unquiet visitor cannot disturb the sweet accord of the minister's family, though the children gather around him, drawn by the tender warmth of his love for them. How vividly he tells the story of his London labours, and of the good countess whom their father loves; or perhaps he recounts his travels among the wild forests and the tall red men of the New World, to which they listen with eager interest; or perhaps he discourses with the parents upon the marvellous works of God, or urges upon the young men of the academy the glorious gospel of his blessed Lord, But private ministrations are not for him. On a Tuesday morning we find him preaching to Doddridge's family, and in the afternoon to above two thousand people in the neighbouring field.

Hervey comes to welcome him, *James Hervey*, one of the Oxford band, now curate in the little village of Western Flavel, so near Northampton that he and Doddridge may often thread the green lanes to each other's houses and take sweet counsel in heavenly things. Hervey is pale and attenuated, but great men find their way to his retired church, for his works are admired among the literary circles of the land. In America he is best known as the author of

"*Meditations in a Graveyard*," once a popular little volume, but now cast in the shade less for the serious tone of it, than for its airy flights of style. Hervey's heart glows while Whitefield talks.

"Surely, I never spent a more delightful evening," exclaimed he, "or saw one that seemed to make nearer approaches to the felicity of heaven. A gentleman of great worth and rank invited us to his house and gave us an elegant treat; but how mean was his provision, how coarse his delicacies, compared with the fruit of my friend's lips. They dropped as a honeycomb, and were a well of life."

Dr Stonehouse is also of the company, once Doddridge's beloved family physician, now a physician of souls. An avowed infidel when he first came to Northampton, the preaching, conversation, writings, and counsels both of Doddridge and Hervey led him to reconsider the ground upon which he stood, discover his perilous condition, and flee to Jesus Christ for refuge from the wrath to come. He afterwards settled at Great and Little Cheveril, Wiltshire, where he became the spiritual guide of Hannah More, and the "Mr Johnson" of her admirable and far-famed tract, "*The Shepherd of Salisbury Plain*." After the death of his wife he married Miss Ekins, a tenderly beloved ward of Dr Doddridge, "whose account of her expenses and estate was so just," says the husband on receiving the property of his bride, "that he really did not do justice to himself, in consequence of which we made his widow a handsome present for his undercharges."

Meanwhile Lady Huntingdon is at Ashby de la Zouch, in Leicestershire, one of the manors belonging to Lord Huntingdon's family, a day's journey from Northampton, if the lumbering vehicles of a hundred years ago could make fifty miles a day. Here were the ladies Hastings, Frances, Anne, and Betty. After a while, Doddridge pays her a visit. On Sabbath forenoon he preached, while her domestic chaplain read the service; in the evening the order was reversed, Doddridge prayed and the chaplain preached. "This is a true catholic spirit," exclaims the countess, "that wishes well to the cause of Christ in every denomination. I wish all the dissenting ministers were like-minded, less attached to little punctilios, and more determined to publish the glorious gospel wherever men are assembled to hear, whether in a church, a meeting-house, a field, or a barn – less anxious to convince their brethren in errors of discipline, and more solicitous to gather souls to Christ."

Whitefield in his rounds at length halts at Ashby. "And Ashby Place is like a Bethel," he exclaims; "we have the sacrament every morning, heavenly conversation all day, and preaching at night. This is to live at court indeed." Does not this picture remind us of the primitive Christians, when they continued daily with one accord in the temple, breaking bread from house to house, eating their meat with gladness and singleness of heart, and praising God?

But the spirit and the preaching of Ashby Place did not suit the humour of the neighbourhood. Riotous proceedings took place on various occasions, inflamed, it was said, by the dissenters; perhaps Whitefield comes nearer the truth when he exclaims, "Alas, how great and irreconcilable is the enmity of the serpent." The countess' house is threatened with ruin, and some persons on their way home narrowly escaped being murdered. "Ungrateful Ashby," cries Whitefield, "O that thou knewest the day of thy visitation. I shall be glad to hear what becomes of the rioters. O that your ladyship may live to see many of those Ashby stones become children to Abraham."

To Lady Gertrude Hotham, one of his London converts, he wrote, "Good Lady Huntingdon is weak in body, but strong in grace. Thousands and thousands flock to hear the Word twice every day, and the power of God has attended it in a glorious manner. But the good people of Ashby were so kind as to mob round her ladyship's door while the gospel was preaching. Ashby is not worthy of so rich a pearl. You and Lady Fanny were constantly remembered at Ashby at the holy table."

Whitefield stayed here a fortnight, continuing instant in season and out of season in his Master's work, when he took leave and pushed on towards the north. As mails were not carried by coaches in England until nearly thirty years after this time, we may suppose there was little public accommodation for travellers. People went in their own conveyances. Let us take a look at Whitefield, as his carriage drives out of Ashby on the road to Nottingham, drawn by a favourite pair of handsome black horses, doing credit to their keeping at the Ashby stables. It was on this journey, while he was preaching at Kendal, surrounded by a listening multitude, that some of the baser sort, honouring the preacher in their own way, entered the barn where his carriage was housed, hacked the leather, abused the trimmings, and cut off the horses' tails. "Still," he observes, "God vouchsafes to prosper the gospel plough. Such an entrance has been made at Kendal as could not have been expected. The people are importunate that I should return again, and the power of the Lord has been wonderfully displayed."

At Nottingham, he was attended by great multitudes, who thronged every avenue to the place appointed for him to preach in; in some places, "Satan rallied," he says, "giving notice of me by calling the people to a bear-baiting: a drum is beat, and men are called to the market-place; but the arrows of the Lord can disperse them." It was at Rotherham that several young men met at a tavern, and undertook on a wager to see who could best mimic him; each in turn mounted the table, and opening a Bible, entertained his companions at the expense of everything sacred. A youth by the name of Thorpe was to close the scene; and he exclaimed, on taking his stand, "I shall beat you all." Opening the Bible, his eye fell on the solemn sentence, "Except ye repent, ye shall all likewise perish." It pierced the young man's soul. The truth mastered him. He spoke, but it was like a dying man to dying men. A profound seriousness spread over the company, and those who came to scoff went away to weep. He afterwards became a preacher, and for many years faithfully ministered in holy things; and his son, Rev William Thorpe, was for a long time one of the stated supplies of the Whitefield chapel in London.

Whitefield visited Aberford, the residence of Ingham and Lady Margaret, where Ingham and Grimshaw joined him on his tour in Yorkshire. From Leeds he writes to Lady Huntingdon, "Last night I preached to many, many thousands, and this morning also at five o'clock. Methinks I am now got into another climate. It must be a warm one, where there are so many of God's people. Our Pentecost is to be kept at Mr Grimshaw's." While at Haworth, Mr Grimshaw's curacy, the Lord's Supper was frequently administered not only to the stated communicants, but to hundreds from other quarters, who resorted hither on these solemn occasions, when it seemed emphatically, that the "Spirit was poured out from on high." "Pen," he writes to Hervey, "cannot well describe what glorious scenes have opened in Yorkshire. Since I was in Ashby, perhaps seventy or eighty thousand have attended the Word preached in divers places. At Haworth, on Whit-Sunday, the church was thrice filled with communicants. It was a precious season."

After travelling through different parts of Lancashire, Westmoreland, and Cumberland, accompanied by Ingham and one or two other kindred spirits, he departs for Scotland; while we return to Ashby, and find Hervey there, among other guests. How feeble is he. Dr Stonehouse can administer nothing for his relief, but advises him to go to London by easy stages, and try the effect of a change of air; and Lady Huntingdon urges it. The next winter finds him lodged not with "his brother after the flesh," but with "the brother of his heart," Mr Whitefield, at his house near Moorfields. Lady Huntingdon commends the invalid to the kind notice of her female friends; at the house of Lady Fanny Shirley and Lady Gertrude Hotham, he preaches as often as his strength admits, and it was to the former that he dedicates his new volume, "*Theron and Aspasio.*"

Early in the month of October, Whitefield comes back to Ashby, after long ranging about, as he says, to see who would believe the gospel report.

"Your kind letter," he answers Doddridge, "finds me happy at our good Lady Huntingdon's, whose path shines brighter and brighter till the perfect day. Gladly shall I call upon you again, if the Lord spares my life; but in the meanwhile, I shall not fail to pray that the work of our common Lord may more and more prosper in your hand. I thank you a thousand times for your kindness to the chief of sinners, and assure you, reverend sir, the affection is reciprocal. I go with regret from Lady Huntingdon. Do come and see her soon."

There were five clergymen now beneath her hospitable roof, "and it is a time of refreshing from the presence of our God," she writes to her aunt, Lady Fanny. "Several of our little circle have been wonderfully filled with the love of God, and have had joy unspeakable and full of glory. It is impossible to conceive more real happiness than Lady Frances enjoys. Dear Mr Whitefield's sermons and conversation are close, searching, experimental, awful, and awakening. Surely God is wonderfully with him."

Whitefield now returned to London. Lady Huntingdon remained with her family at Ashby Place. Her health is delicate: "Dr Stonehouse still administers to her in bodily things, though he has just taken the cure of souls. He is thrown much into the society of those who are movers and actors in the great religious movements of the day, some of whom are among his choicest friends; yet he seems to have felt a strong repugnance to the term 'Methodist,' and perhaps it was in reference to his timid conservatism upon this point, that Lady Huntingdon urges, 'Go forth boldly, fear not the reproach of men, and preach the inestimable gift of God to impotent sinners.'"

"For Christ's sake, dear Mr Hervey," wrote Whitefield, "exhort Dr Stonehouse, now that he hath taken the gown, to 'play the man;'" and to the doctor himself he says, "I have thought of you and prayed for you much, since we parted at Northampton. How wonderfully doth the Lord Jesus watch over you. How sweetly doth he lead you out of temptation. O follow his leadings, my dear friend, and let every, even the most beloved Isaac, be immediately sacrificed for God. God's law is our rule, and God will have all the heart or none. Agags will plead, but they must be hewn in pieces. May you quit yourself like a man, and in every respect behave like a good soldier of Jesus Christ."

"Allow me to express my heartfelt gratitude for the very faithful manner in which you have placed my serious duties before me," he courteously replies to Lady Huntingdon, "duties high and honourable, but arduous indeed. What holy and excellent examples have I in the exalted piety and ministerial fidelity of Doddridge, Hervey, and Hartley, and the undaunted zeal of that great apostle, Mr Whitefield. May I be a follower of them as they are of Christ, and whatever little differences may exist between us, may we all finally meet before the throne of God and the Lamb."

Dr Stonehouse is said to have become one of the most elegant preachers of the kingdom, and for the grace of propriety perhaps he was mainly indebted to Garrick, whose famous criticism will bear repeating.

Being once engaged to read prayers and preach at a church in London, he prevailed upon Garrick to go with him. After the service, the actor asked the preacher what particular business he had to do when the duty was over.

"None," said the other.

"I thought you had," said Garrick, "on seeing you enter the reading-desk in such a hurry. Nothing can be more indecent than to see a clergyman set about sacred business as if he were a tradesman, and go into church as if he wanted to get out of it as soon as possible." He next asked the doctor what books he had before him.

"Only the Bible and Prayer-book."

"*Only* the Bible and Prayer-book?" replied the player; "why, you tossed them backwards and forwards, and turned the leaves as carelessly, as if they were those of a daybook and ledger."

The doctor acknowledged the force of the criticism by henceforth avoiding the faults it was designed to correct. Might not many a young preacher of our own day wisely profit by the same?

6
Doddridge

ONE of the finest expositions of Dr Doddridge's own principles, of which it can justly be said he was a "living epistle," we find in a sermon of his delivered in January, 1750, before a meeting of ministers at Creaton, in Northamptonshire, upon *"Christian Candour and Unanimity."*

"To agree in our sentiments as to every point of doctrine or discipline, or as to the authority or expediency of every rite of worship that may be in question, is absolutely impossible. The best of men differ – their understandings differ – various associations have been accidentally formed, and different principles have been innocently and perhaps devoutly admitted, which even a course of just and sensible reasoning must necessarily lead to different conclusions. But," says the excellent man, "where we and our brethren agree in attending to the *one thing* which Christianity was designed to teach us, surely *an agreement in that* should unite our hearts, more than any difference consistent with that agreement should divide them. To reverence with filial love the God of heaven, and adore him with integrity of heart; to honour Jesus his Son as the brightest image, subscribing to the truth of all he is known to have revealed, and the authority of all he is apprehended to command; conscientiously to abstain from every known evil, and to practise, as far as human infirmity will admit, the comprehensive precepts of living soberly, righteously, and godly; still looking for the mercy of our Lord Jesus Christ unto eternal life, setting the affections on those great objects which the gospel opens to our view, and finally, being habitually ready to sacrifice life and all its enjoyments to that blessed hope – this, this, my brethren, is the essential character of every Christian; and where we see this, shall we esteem it a difficult thing to live peaceably with him? Shall we esteem it a praise that we do not censure, grieve, or injure him, because he follows not us? Is this the man to be hated and suspected? I will add, Can we refuse to embrace and esteem him, merely because he worships in another assembly, or according to a different form; because he expresses his apprehensions about some of the doctrines in different words; because he cannot see all we think we discern in some passages of Scripture, or because he imagines he sees something which we discern not? And is it, after all, so great a matter to love a character which, amidst all its imperfections, is in general so justly amiable? Nay, instead of thinking much of any act of kindness, ought we not rather to lament that we can do no more? Ought we not rather to endeavour to supply in our fervent prayers to God the lack of that further service which Christian benevolence dictates, but which the narrow limits of our condition or our nature will not allow us to perform?

"Methinks the matter might be safely rested here." And yet he finds it good to illustrate and enforce his principles by many winning arguments; and more powerfully still did he commend them by his own example of loving fellowship with Hervey and Romaine, with Whitefield and Ingham, and indeed with all of whatever name who could reciprocate such charity. May not Doddridge thus speak to us? Let us filially contemplate this phase of his character, if haply we may catch his spirit and profit by his teachings.

On being published, this discourse was dedicated to Lady Huntingdon, "that eminent example of Christian candour here recommended, and of every other virtue and grace which can inspire, support, and adorn it."

In June we find Doddridge at Ashby, and from a letter written to his beloved pupil and ministerial brother, Rev Benjamin Fawcett of Kidderminster, we find some notes of pleasant memory.

"Lady Huntingdon, for whom I desired your prayers, is wonderfully recovered. She walked with me in the garden and park, and almost wearied me, such is her recruit of strength; but the strength of her soul is amazing. I think I never saw so much of the image of God in any woman upon earth. Were I to write what I know of her, it would fill your heart with wonder, joy, and praise. She desired me to educate a lad for the dissenting ministry at her expense, till he be fit to come to my academy; and this is but one of a multitude of good works which she is continually performing. I must tell you, however, one observation which struck me much: 'None,' said she, 'know how to prize Christ, but those who are zealous in good works. Men know not till they try, what imperfect things these best works are, and how deficient we are in them; and the experience of that sweetness that attends their performance, makes me more sensible of those obligations to Him whose grace is the principle of them in our hearts.' She has God dwelling in her, and she is ever bearing her testimony to the present salvation he has given us, and to the fountain of living waters which she feels springing up in her soul; so that she knows the divine original of the promises before the performance of them to her, as she knows God to be her Creator by the life he has given her.

"As I was setting out on my blessed journey to her, for such indeed it was, yesterday was seven-night, a terrible accident happened to my study, which might have been attended with fatal consequences. I had been sealing a letter with a little roll of wax, and I thought I had blown it out, when fanned by the motion of the air as I arose in haste, it was rekindled. It burnt about a quarter of an hour, while we were at prayer, and would have gone on perhaps to have consumed the closet and the house, had not my opposite neighbour seen the flame and given the alarm.

"When I came up I found my desk, which was covered with papers, burning like an altar: many letters, papers of memoranda, and schemes of sermons were consumed. My book of accounts was on fire, and a volume of the *Family Expositor*, the original manuscript from Corinthians to Ephesians, surrounded by flames and drenched with melted wax; and yet, so did God moderate the rage of this element, and determine in his providence the time of our entrance, that not one account is rendered uncertain, nor is one line which had not been transcribed destroyed in the manuscript. Observe, my dear friend, His hand, and magnify the Lord with me."

In the preface to this volume of the *Family Expositor*, he writes, "Well may it be said, 'Is not this a brand plucked out of the burning?' A fire was kindled among my papers which endangered the utter ruin of my affairs. Everything must have gone, had it not been for the glance of an eye by which an opposite neighbour discovered it. I desire now to leave it upon record, that I now have received this wonderful mercy from the Lord, and would consider it as an engagement to devote all I have to him with greater zeal."

In December of this year Lady Huntingdon had a dangerous illness, which greatly alarmed her friends. She was at Ashby with her daughters and sisters, the Ladies Hastings. This month Dr Doddridge is also called to St Albans to preach the funeral-sermon of his almost father, Dr Samuel Clarke, author of "*The Promises*," a man highly venerated by his brethren and gratefully beloved by Doddridge.

"I want to be a minister," was the chief desire of a young lad, many years before this time. He was an orphan and poor, for all the little patrimony left him by his father was lost by his guardian. He left school and went to his sister, but her income was too small to render him effectual aid. He loved study, and his uppermost wish was to preach the gospel, yet darkness was on the way. A rich lady having learned something of his cleverness, offered to pay his expenses at Oxford, provided he would enter the English church. He was very grateful to this lady, but he felt constrained to refuse the offer, for he revered the faith of his fathers, and chose rather to suffer constraint and reproach with the dissenters, than to dwell in the sumptuous tents of the establishment.

Troubled and anxious, he thought he would venture to call upon a learned minister in the neighbourhood, lay his case before him, and ask his advice. The gentleman received the poor lad coolly, and spoke no word of encouragement. He advised him to choose another calling, and think no more of preaching. Disheartened more and more, he turned away from the house sorrowfully. "Try the law," said some of his friends, and not long afterwards they procured him a suitable situation in an office. There seemed to be nothing else for him to do; but before the final decision, the young man set apart one morning especially to seek the direction of God in this matter.

While engaged in prayer, the postman knocked at the door. He brought the young man a letter. It was from an early friend of his father, who, having learned his destitute condition, offered, if he were still intent upon the work of the ministry, to take him under his care and assist him in his studies. What a precious letter it was! "This," he exclaimed with heartfelt gratitude, "I look upon almost as an answer from heaven, and while I live I shall always adore so seasonable an opening of divine Providence. I have sought God's direction in all this matter, and I hope I have had it, and I beg he would make me an instrument of doing much good in the world."

His desires were gratified, for God enabled him not only to become a useful and beloved minister himself, but to train up many others for the same holy calling. What a blessing waits on those who wait on God. This young lad was *Philip Doddridge*, and the timely friend, good Dr Clarke of St Albans, whose death he is now called to mourn. An uninterrupted friendship had ever subsisted between them, the elder rejoicing in the ripe and useful manhood of his once orphan charge, and the younger holding in grateful memory the friend who appeared to him in the hour of his need.

On this journey to St Albans, to officiate at the funeral services, in the raw and chilly weather of an English December, Doddridge took a severe cold, which hung about him all winter.

Lady Huntingdon continues ill. "I fear we shall soon lose her too," he says, "but the Lord liveth, and blessed be our Rock." At the beginning of the new year, 1751, she declined so rapidly that Whitefield was sent for in haste from London. "I rode post to Ashby," he said, "not knowing whether I should find good Lady Huntingdon alive. Blessed be God, she is somewhat better, and I trust will not die, but live, and abound more and more in the work of the Lord. Entreat all our friends to pray for her. Indeed she is worthy."

A few hours before Whitefield reached Ashby, Lady Frances Hastings was suddenly removed to that

"*Land of pure delight,*
Where saints immortal reign."

Her age was fifty-seven. In all things she adorned the doctrine of her Saviour. Her gentleness and sincerity endeared her to a large circle of friends, and heavenly-mindedness made her a choice spirit among the people of God; while a multitude of the neighbouring poor attended her funeral, weeping "for the good works and alms-deeds which she had done."

"She seemed, as it were, to smile at death," wrote Whitefield to Lady Mary Hamilton, her intimate friend, "and may be said, I trust truly, to have fallen asleep in Jesus. Lady Betty is more affected than I ever saw her. Lady Anne bears up pretty well; while Lady Huntingdon rejoices at the thought of her sister's being so quickly translated out of this house of bondage into the glorious liberty of the sons of God."

Everybody advises her ladyship to take a journey to Bristol, for the benefit of the waters, which she hopes to do.

After Whitefield left, Dr Stonehouse came to Ashby, where he remained until the invalid could be removed to Bristol Hot-Wells, whither she went in the beginning of March. Just before going, Doddridge seems to have paid her a visit, for we hear her exclaiming, "How holy, how humble is that excellent man! And what divine words fell from his lips at the last sacramental feast! How close and searching were his addresses! I think I was scarce ever so happy before. He and Dr Stonehouse have preached alternately every evening. I trust my journey to Bristol will be for good. O that my health and strength may be wholly employed for that blessed Redeemer who has done such great things for me."

A few weeks find her much recruited in strength, and she is now at Bristol, interesting herself and her friends to procure subscribers for the last three volumes of "*The Family Expositor*," just completed. This Doddridge esteemed his "capital work," which he began to prepare on his first entrance into the ministry, and always kept in view through all his subsequent studies. On transmitting to him a long list of additional subscribers, "I have the unspeakable pleasure of communicating intelligence that will rejoice my much-esteemed friend," she says. "Most earnestly do I pray the Lord of all lords to prolong your valuable life, and give you strength and abilities for the publication of a work so calculated to promote the glory of his name, and the everlasting good of mankind."

Alas, there were symptoms that this valuable life was on its wane. His early winter cold has never left him. Months pass away and there is no abatement of his cough. Anxiety and fear creep into the bosom of his family. The skill of his physician seems baffled. The tenderest nursing loses its healing power. Everything is expected from the benign influences of spring; and while hope alternates with fear in the hearts of his friends, he is urged, as milder weather approaches, to leave his laborious charge at Northampton, and try a change of air and scene.

"Use all means," wrote one in impassioned accents, "use all means to repair your frame and prolong your usefulness; this is not only needful for Northampton and its adjacent towns and villages, but desirable to us all and beneficial to our whole interests. Stay, Doddridge, O stay and strengthen our hands, whose shadows grow long. Fifty is but the height of usefulness, vigour, and honour. Providence hath not directed thee yet on whom to drop thy mantle. Who shall instruct our youth, fill our vacant churches, animate our associations, and diffuse a spirit of piety, moderation, candour, and charity throughout our villages and churches, and a spirit of prayer and supplication into our towns and cities, when thou art removed from us? Especially, who shall rescue us from the bondage of systems, party opinions, empty, useless speculations, and fashionable forms and phrases, and point out to us the simple, intelligible, consistent, uniform religion of our Lord and Saviour?"

With the soft influences of the season, and the exhilaration produced by easy journeying through some of the most beautiful parts of the kingdom, the invalid seemed to revive; those less acquainted with the flattering nature of his disease, even looked for recovery, but every auspicious token was speedily dissipated when with the increasing warm weather he grew more languid and feeble. A sea-voyage is now the last sad resort, and his physician advises a trip to Lisbon. The expense being beyond his limited means, Lady Huntingdon generously contributed one hundred pounds, which, with the aid rendered by Lady Fanny Shirley, Lady Chesterfield, and a few others, was raised to three hundred; "and this," she says, "with what his friends among the dissenters may collect, will, I hope, be of essential service in procuring him every comfort which his almost helpless state requires."

Early in September we learn she is at Bath, in devoted attendance upon Dr Doddridge, who is in a deep-seated consumption, but who is to set out in a few days in order to embark at Falmouth for Lisbon, whence Dr Oliver thinks "he will never return."

The tenderest and deepest solicitude is felt by his many friends all over the kingdom; numerous letters daily arrive filled with anxious inquiries after his health; and affection and skill do their utmost to relieve him. "My soul," he says, "is vigorous and healthy, notwithstanding the hastening decay of this frail and tottering body. It is not for the love of sunshine, or the variety of meats, that I desire life; but, if it please God, that I may render him a little more service." How did he regard the approaching voyage?

"The means I am about pursuing," he hoarsely whispers, "to save life, so far as I am solely concerned, are to my apprehension worse than death. My profuse night-sweats are very weakening to my material frame; but the most distressing nights to this frail body have been as the *beginning of heaven* to my soul. God hath, as it were, let heaven down upon me in those nights of weakness and waking. Blessed be his name."

Yet friends urge it, and he consents. On the morning of his departure, Lady Huntingdon entered his room and found him weeping over the open Bible lying before him.

"You are in tears, sir," she said.

"I am weeping, madam," replied the doctor in a faint, yet calm tone, "but they are tears of joy and comfort. I can give up my country, my friends, my relatives, into the hands of God; and as to myself, I can as well go to heaven from Lisbon, as from my own study at Northampton."

"I see indeed no prospect of recovery," again said the almost dying man, "yet my heart rejoiceth in my God and my Saviour, and I can call him, under this failure of everything else, my strength and everlasting portion. God hath indeed been wonderfully good to me, but I am less than the least of his mercies, less than the least hope of his children. Adored be his grace for whatever it hath wrought by me."

After a fatiguing journey of ten days, owing to the wetness of the season and the bad state of the roads, he reached Falmouth, and was hospitably received into the house of Dr Turner, a clergyman of the English church. On the night before embarking, some of his worst symptoms, which had been for a while checked, returned with great violence, so that his wife entreated that the voyage might be given up. "The die is cast, and I will go," was the quiet answer.

"On the 30th of September," writes one of him, "accompanied by his anxious wife and servant, he sailed from Falmouth; and, revived by the soft breezes and the ship's stormless progress, he sat in his easy-chair in the cabin enjoying the brightest thoughts of all his life. 'Such transporting views of the heavenly world is my Father now indulging me with, as no words can express,' was his frequent exclamation to the tender partner of his voyage; and when the ship was gliding up the Tagus, and Lisbon with its groves and gardens and sunny towers stood before them, so animating was the spectacle, that affection hoped he might yet recover. That hope was vain. Bad symptoms soon came on, and the chief advantage of the change was, that it perhaps rendered dissolution more easy. On the 26th of October, 1751, at the age of 50, he ceased from his labours, and soon after was laid in the burying-ground of the English factory."

"God is all-sufficient, and my only hope," writes the afflicted wife to her family at Northampton. "Oh, my dear children, help me to praise Him. Such supports, such consolations, such comforts has he granted, that my mind at times is astonished and is ready to burst into songs of praise under its most exquisite distress. As to outward comforts, God has withheld no good thing from me but has given me all the assistance and all the supports that the tenderest friendship was capable of affording me, and which I think my dear Northampton friends could not have exceeded. Their prayers are not lost. I doubt not I am reaping the benefit of them, and I hope that you will do the same."

Such is the eloquent utterance of the believer. "I will bless the Lord at all times; his praise shall continually be in my mouth. Oh, taste and see that the Lord is good: blessed is the man that trusteth in him. There is no want to them that fear him."

Nor can we let pass the sound preacher, the successful writer, the beloved pastor, without a grateful tribute to the memory of Doddridge as the sweet lyrist of God's people. Has he not given a voice to the most cherished emotions of the soul? Has he not been with us on our covenant-day, and with exquisite pathos bid

– *"the glowing heart rejoice
And tell its raptures all abroad"*?

Beset with foes and ready to faint by the way, world-weary, have not his stirring words, come to us like the breath of heaven?

*"A cloud of witnesses around,
Hold thee in full survey:
Forget the steps already trod.
And onward urge thy way."*

Has he not stayed the tear in its fountain by the exhilarating prospect,

*"Fast as ye bring the night of death,
Ye bring eternal day"*?

And he must ever be a sweet singer to the Israel of God until the coming of the new Jerusalem, where is no more death, neither sorrow nor crying, neither any more pain, for the former things have passed away.

7

The Tabernacle – Venn – Preaching Tours

THE present inhabitants in and around Moorfields in London would hardly be willing to acknowledge the sorry figure which that area made a little more than a hundred years ago. This tract of land, just beyond the limits of the old city wall, was, as its name indicates, a marsh, and impassable the greater part of the year. Having been partially drained, a brick kiln was erected, and the first bricks used in London were manufactured there. Afterwards it was a field for the practice of archery, when it was laid out in walks and called the City Mall. Though improved in name and appearance, it became the rallying ground of all the rabble in London; wrestlers, boxers, and mountebanks, the idle, the dissolute, and profane held here their daily and nightly revels. It appeared in fact to be one of the strongholds of Satan, and therefore became a most tempting and important point of attack for the daring eloquence of Whitefield. All London rang one day with the announcement that Whitefield would preach the day following at Moorfields; this was in January, 1739.

"The thing being strange and new," says Gillies, "he found, on coming out of the coach, an incredible number of people assembled. Many told him he would never come out of that place alive. He went in however between two friends, who by the pressure of the crowd were soon parted from him entirely, and obliged to leave him to the mercy of the rabble. But these, instead of hurting him, formed a lane for him, and carried him along to the middle of the fields, where a table had been placed; this however having been broken by the crowd, he mounted a wall and preached to an exceeding great multitude in tones so melting, that his words drew tears and groans from the most abandoned. Moorfields became henceforth one of the principal scenes of his triumphs. Thirty thousand people sometimes gathered to hear him, and generous contributions here flowed in for his orphan-house at Bethesda. On one occasion twenty pounds were received in half-pennies, more than one person was able to carry away, and enough to put one out of conceit with a specie currency."

Before Whitefield went to Georgia, in 1738, a temporary shed had been roughly thrown up to screen the people from the cold, and called a Tabernacle, in allusion to the movable sanctuary of the Israelites in the wilderness. A more spacious edifice was now projected. The matter first came up for discussion in the summer of 1751, when Doddridge, Stonehouse, Hervey, and Whitefield happened to meet together at Lady Huntingdon's in Ashby. During the following winter Whitefield began to make collections for the object, and on almost its first presentation at London nine hundred pounds were subscribed. "But," he says, "on the principle that burned children dread the fire, I do not mean to begin until I get one thousand in hand, and then to contract at a certain sum for the whole." The fact was, Whitefield had often been in great straits for the support of his orphan-house over the sea, "for I forgot," he tells us, "to recollect that Professor Franke built in Glaucha, in a populous country, and that I was building at the very tail of the world." In accordance with this prudent resolution, it was not until March, 1753, that he writes to Charles Wesley, "On Tuesday morning the first brick of our new Tabernacle was laid with awful solemnity. I preached from Exodus: 'In all places where I record my name, I will come unto thee and bless thee.' The wall is now about a yard high. The building is to be eighty feet square. It is on the old spot. We have bought the house, and if we finish what we have begun, shall be rent free for forty-six years."

In June it was ready for the opening services, and though capable of holding four thousand people, was crowded to suffocation. Whitefield was now solicited to hold public services at the west end of London, and Long Acre chapel, then under the charge of a dissenter, was offered for his use. An unruly rabble tried to drive the preacher from his post; but a running fire of brickbats, broken glass, bells, drums, and clappers, neither annoyed nor frightened the intrepid evangelist, nor did a hierarchical interference which followed hard after, prohibiting his preaching in an incorporated chapel. "I hope you will not look upon it as contumacy," said Whitefield to the

bishop, "if I persist in prosecuting my design until I am more particularly apprised wherein I have erred. I trust the irregularity I am
charged with will appear justifiable to every lover of English liberty,
and what is all to me, be approved at the awful and impartial tribunal
of the great Bishop and Shepherd of souls."

"My greatest distress," he says to Lady Huntingdon in the course
of these proceedings, "is so to act as to avoid rashness on the one
hand and timidity on the other;" and this shows, what in truth his
whole life showed, an entire absence of that malignant element of
fanaticism which courts opposition and revels in it.

Determined not to be beaten from his ground, yet hoping to
escape some of its annoyances, Whitefield resolved to build a chapel
of his own. Hence arose Tottenham Court chapel, which went by
the name of "Whitefield's soul-trap." "I pray the Friend of sinners
to make it a soul-trap indeed to many wandering creatures," said he.
"My constant work is preaching fifteen times a week. Conviction and
conversion go on here, for God hath met us in our new building."

This chapel was opened in November, 1756, according to the forms
of the Church of England, and licensed under the Toleration Act, as
other houses of prayer. Twelve alms-houses and a chapel-house were
added two years after. The lease granted by General George Fitzroy
to Mr Whitefield having expired in 1828, it was purchased by the
trustees and reopened in 1830, when Rev William Jay preached the
re-opening sermon. The chapel at present is a handsome building,
the exterior coated with stucco and ornamented with pilasters; the
interior is neat and tasteful. Its present pulpit is the same in which
Whitefield preached. Among the monumental tablets, you read the
names of Whitefield, Toplady, and Joss.

It was before the new Tabernacle was completed that we find
Whitefield, in one of his summer tours, revisiting Scotland, and dom-
iciled at the hospitable mansion of Mr James Nimmo at Edinburgh,
a gentleman of high birth and unaffected piety. This was his third
visit to the north, the first of which took place in 1741; and greater
multitudes than ever now flocked to hear him. While in Edinburgh,
though much indisposed by chills and fever, he continued to preach
twice a day, early in the morning and at six in the evening. "Your
ladyship's health," he says in a letter to Lady Huntingdon, "is drunk
and inquired after every day. Mr Nimmo and his family are in the

number of those who are left in Sardis, and have not defiled their garments." A letter from Lady Jane, who is the friend and correspondent of Lady Huntingdon, reveals to us not only a lively picture of the religious movements at the Scottish capital, but the high consideration with which Lady Huntingdon is regarded by the people of God in that quarter.

"Accept my thanks for your very obliging message by Mr Whitefield, and I hope to avail myself of your very kind offer the first time I go to London with Mr Nimmo. Your ladyship will rejoice to hear what crowds flock to hear Mr Whitefield. The energy and power of the gospel word is truly remarkable. Dear Lady Frances Gardiner is very active in bringing people to hear him. There is a great awakening among all classes. Truth is great and will prevail, notwithstanding all manner of evil is spoken against it. The fields are more than white and ready unto the harvest in Scotland. Many prayers are offered up for your ladyship, and many bless God for your sending your chaplain into these parts. The infinitely condescending Redeemer vouchsafes to bless your labours for the good of souls in England, and your ladyship will shortly have my native country to add to the brilliancy of that diadem which will adorn your brow in the great day of the Lord. I blush and am confounded when I think to what little purpose I have lived. I beg, dear madam, you will pray for me. I feel under manifold obligations to you, and hope to spend an eternity with you in praising that grace and love that has plucked us as brands from the burning. Mr Nimmo begs his most cordial salutations to you, yours, and all who love our Lord Jesus Christ; and wishing you the best of blessings, I subscribe myself, my dear madam, your ladyship's, most affectionately in our common Lord.

"JANE NIMMO"

About this time two gentlemen came from America to solicit contributions for Princeton college. These were Mr Allen and Colonel Williams. They brought letters of introduction from General Belcher of New Jersey to Lady Huntingdon, who collected considerable sums for the object. Mr Allen died in two months after his arrival of a disease called the jail fever, first known in 1750, at the summer session of Old Bailey. Three years afterwards, Messrs. Tennent and Davies were sent over to reawaken the interest and further the cause.

Among the publications of the day appeared "*Theron and Aspasio,*" by Hervey, in which the doctrines of the cross were illustrated and enforced in the form of dialogue. "Thank God for the masterly defence of them in these dialogues," exclaimed Romaine.

The book was dedicated to Lady Fanny Shirley, who became the appreciating patron and warm friend of the invalid and retiring preacher. Though long gone by, these dialogues are still well worth reading, both for the truths they teach and the spirit which they breathe. Let us go and see Hervey on a Sunday.

"Last Sabbath-day, after preaching in the morning at Olney, with three others I rode to hear one Mr Hervey, a minister of the Church of England, who preached at Collingtree, and to my great surprise as well as satisfaction, having never seen such a thing before in prayer-time, instead of singing psalms they sang two of Dr Watts' hymns, the clerk giving them out line by line: after prayer, without going out of the desk, the minister put off his surplice and turned to the fifteenth chapter of Matthew, which was the second lesson of the day, and told the people what pleasure had occurred in his mind while reading the parable of our Saviour's feeding the four thousand men, besides women and children, with seven loaves and a few little fishes: he then spoke in a plain, simple manner about it, and afterwards spiritualised it by observing what great things the Lord sometimes does by small things and weak instruments. And then, without going up into the pulpit, he turned to the fifth chapter of the Ephesians, and read the twenty-fifth, twenty-sixth, and twenty-seventh verses, and very sweetly and clearly he spoke from them; showing the meaning of those words in the creed, *I believe in the holy catholic church,* wherein he observed, They do not believe in the church, as in God Almighty and in his Son Jesus Christ our Lord; but the meaning, he observed, was, I believe God has a holy catholic church; and the word *catholic* signifies *universal;* that there always was, now is, and will be a church of Christ. He then from the holy Word showed who were the members of this church; such as were cleansed, washed, or justified from their sins in the blood of our Lord Jesus Christ; and here he spoke very clearly to the people, and told them that *all* were not of or in this church, which he compared to Noah and his family in the ark being safe, when all the rest were drowned in the deluge. In like manner he showed, notwithstanding their coming to that place or building, if they were not members of that church he had been describing, by being united to Jesus Christ by faith, they, as the people out of the ark, must perish at last. And as he had been telling them who were members of this church, he spoke in a humble way of himself as being an unworthy member thereof. And now having shown what was meant by the church, and who were its members, he showed lastly, from the words that were read, what were the church's privileges. Thus far I have been particular, for such a way of proceeding in the Church of England seems wonderful to me. But what shall we say? God is no respecter of persons, neither of places. This Mr Hervey expounds every Wednesday night, catechises the children, and meets some people on Tuesdays and Thursdays in or near the parish where he lives."

Surely here is in very deed a servant of the true spiritual church of the Redeemer, bought with his own precious blood.

Rev Bryan Broughton, secretary of the Society for Promoting Christian Knowledge, was also one of the original Oxford band. Now living at London, college friendships are kept alive, and he is still the friend and associate of Whitefield and the Wesleys. There came to our house, he says, the newly-appointed curate of St Matthew's, a young man, whose fresh and earnest spirit was prepared to regard the new religious movements of the time with candid and inquiring interest. "Are these things from God?" he asked reverently.

His name is *Henry Venn*, whose *"Complete Duty of Man"* is now among the choice and sterling books of our religious libraries. Law's *"Serious Call"* had made a deep impression upon his mind, and he was endeavouring to meet its stern and uncompromising demands upon his moral nature. Like the Wesleys at Oxford, he prescribed to himself a rigid course of fasting and prayer. He determined resolutely to grapple with the evil of his nature, and compel his rebel affections to do homage to their Lord. But the course thus marked out could not meet his wants. No self-inflictions could reach the necessities of the case. He now became acquainted with Whitefield, Lady Huntingdon, and others like-minded, who from their own fervent experience could point him to *"the Lamb of God, which taketh away the sin of the world."* A severe and long-continued illness, which broke in upon his public labours, gave him time for deep searching of heart and uninterrupted meditation upon divine truth. His views of doctrine grew clearer, and salvation by the blood of Christ as the grand central doctrine of the Scriptures, became distinct and precious to his soul. When he again went forth to his ministry, he went in the might of a crucified and risen Saviour, deeply imbued with that spirit of prayer and holy consecration which made his conversation, his preaching, and his writings so eminently useful in his day. Soon after his recovery he accompanied Whitefield upon a preaching tour into Gloucestershire, where they proclaimed to immense crowds the glad tidings of the gospel. At Clifton they were welcomed and hospitably entertained by Lady Huntingdon, and here Venn met many kindred spirits, whose sympathy and knowledge in divine things quickened and rejoiced his spirit.

In 1759 he received the large and valuable living of Huddersfield in West Yorkshire, one hundred and ninety miles north-west of London, and Mr Venn became the apostle of the region. He was instant in season and out of season, exhorting, rebuking, reproving with all long-suffering and patience.

"Preach Christ crucified as the only foundation of the sinner's hope," wrote Lady Huntingdon to him, "and may your bow abide in strength. Be bold, be firm, be decisive. Let Christ be the Alpha and Omega of all your addresses to your fellow-men, and may the gracious benediction of your heavenly Master rest upon you."

Pastoral fidelity was one of the chief excellences of this man of God. He made frequent visits to all the different hamlets of his extensive parish, collecting together those who could not attend divine worship on the Sabbath, and instructing them from house to house.

"I have delightful accounts from Huddersfield," said his patron, "of the wonderful manner in which the ministry of their faithful and laborious vicar is blessed to that people; and what is gratifying, his health was never better."

We cannot but look with surprise upon the prodigious labours of many in the ministry at this period, when work and health and long life seemed to go hand in hand. Hard roads, rough weather, pressing service, threats, and opposition never daunted, nor discouraged, nor interrupted their labours. They shrank from no toils. "Heart within and God o'erhead," they proved themselves patient and hardy labourers, simple in their habits, strong in faith, and solicitous chiefly about the furtherance of the kingdom of their Lord and Master.

Yorkshire, one of the largest counties of England, is washed by the German ocean, and is divided into east, west, and north ridings. It contains many ranges of high land, and is watered by the Ouse, Don, Humber, and Aire. This was the native county and principal theatre of the labours of *Benjamin Ingham*, one of Wesley's college band. On leaving Oxford in 1734, he went to his mother's house, where he used to collect little companies about the neighbourhood and expound to them the Word of God. With the Wesleys he went to Georgia, and laboured at a small Indian mission a few miles from Savannah. He learned the language, made a grammar, and became deeply interested in the wild sons of the forest. On the return of the brothers to England, he accompanied them, and shortly revisited his native county. At Wakefield, Leeds, and Halifax he preached with marvellous power. This provoked ecclesiastical censure, and he was prohibited the use of the churches throughout the diocese of York. Not at all dismayed or discouraged, he betook himself to the fields, where crowds of hungry hearers hung upon his lips: everywhere the common people heard him gladly; others also were subdued by his searching and personal appeals. The Hastings of Ledstone Hall lent an ear to his instructions, and embraced the truths thus heartily and zealously enforced. In 1741, as has been related, he married Lady Margaret Hastings, Earl Huntingdon's youngest sister, and made his home at Aberford.

Co-worker with Ingham was *William Grimshaw* of Haworth. Haworth is a bleak and unpromising little parish, embracing four hamlets, which afford little to interest the fastidious; but they enclosed the joys and sorrows, the sins and the infirmities of humanity, and this made them worthy of the curate's best endeavours. Besides his Sabbath service, Grimshaw established two circuits, which he went over every week alternately. On what he called his idle week, he preached twelve or fourteen times; his busy week from twenty-four to thirty, going also from house to house, visiting the sick, instructing the ignorant, comforting the sorrowful, and helping the aged towards heaven.

One of the most violent opposers of Grimshaw and Ingham was the vicar of Colne, a town on the borders of Yorkshire. On hearing of the arrival of any of the awakened preachers into his neighbourhood, he used to call the people together by beating a drum in the market-place, and enlisting the mob for the defence of the church: one of his proclamations to this end is a curious specimen of ecclesiastical tactics.

"Notice is hereby given, that if any man be mindful to enlist in his majesty's service, under the command of Rev George White, commander-in-chief, and John Banister, lieutenant-general of his majesty's forces for the defence of the Church of England, and the support of the manufactory in and about Colne, both of which are now in danger, let him repair to the drum-head at the cross, where each man shall receive a pint of ale in advance, and all other proper encouragement."

The reckless fury of a force thus enlisted may be well imagined: the preachers often ran a gauntlet for their lives; they and their congregations were pelted with stones and dirt, trampled into the mud, and beaten without mercy; the constables often rivalling the vicar in his violence and hatred against them.

Newton was much in Yorkshire previous to his own settlement, loving and labouring both with Ingham and Grimshaw. "I forgot to tell you," he writes to a friend, "that I had the honour to appear as a Methodist preacher. I was at Haworth; Mr Grimshaw was present and preached. I love the people called Methodists, and vindicate them from unjust aspersions, and suffer the reproach of the world for being one myself, yet it seems not practicable for me to join them farther than I do; for the present I must try to be useful in private life."

Lady Huntingdon and her chaplains often journeyed during the summer, making their presence a means of religious revival wherever they went. We find her now, in company with Romaine, travelling in Yorkshire, and tarrying at Aberford, guests of the Inghams. Romaine and Ingham, though together at college, knew and cared little for each other then; they now met warm and intrepid champions of the cross. Lady Margaret felt a cordial sympathy for Romaine in his London trials and reverses, and generously eked out his small income from her own purse; while her husband accompanied him on preaching tours throughout the north of England – Romaine preaching wherever he could obtain a pulpit, and Ingham exhorting in chapels and private houses.

At Haworth, a large crowd having assembled, Mr Grimshaw gave out word that "his brother Romaine would preach the glorious gospel from brother Whitefield's pulpit in the graveyard;" and though the announcement did not quite suit the preacher's taste or principles, he felt it was no time for a minister of Christ to stick at forms; Romaine therefore took his stand in that temple not made with hands, and proclaimed the unsearchable riches of Christ.

There is something grand and beautiful in the laborious and unselfish ministrations of the band of preachers who thus went out into the highways and hedges of England, publishing the gospel message as if fresh from Christ and Calvary. We feel there was vitality and power in their utterances, and we almost wish that *we* too might have been there to see and hear. We look around in our own time, and even with all the multiplied apparatus of church extension in our day, all the bustling activity of our societies and anniversaries, the current of our spiritual life seems tame and sluggish compared with the warm and quickened flow of theirs. We cannot help the inquiry, "What was the main element of *their* preaching, which we have not? Where were the hidings of that wondrous power which electrified both England and her colonies? for America also had her Edwards and her Tennents."

It was not learning or logic merely, though some of them were learned and giant men; it was not artistic eloquence, eloquent as they were; nor was it the burning of a sectarian or selfish zeal: it was a profound and vivid sense of sin and redemption, of heaven and hell – in a word, of the stupendous and solemn issues of man's moral history; they *felt* the reality and the grandeur of eternity.

Nurtured and brought up with the Bible, the catechism, or the prayer-book, many men have only a conventional sort of piety: they believe because nobody questions; they preach because it is a profession, and a noble one; they maintain a respectable standing among their fellows; and though in their more spiritual moments they may conceive of that latent heat and hidden power, the divinity which underlies redemptive truths, they yet see only through a glass darkly, and make little progress. Buffetings, aggression, conquest in their Master's service, however they may have been elements in the labours of apostles and reformers, form no part of their inner or outer life – they sail on no such stormy seas. Now let this inherited and passive belief in the truths of Christianity, setting easily upon us like a fashionable garment, become instinct with life – let the curtain of the present and visible world be suddenly rent away, and ourselves and our fellows be seen hastening to eternal joy or remediless woe, and from that hour onward we are altered beings.

It was this quickened apprehension of revealed truth, this deeper intuition into man's lost estate, which made Paul and Peter, Luther and Calvin, Whitefield and Wesley, Edwards and Tennent what they were; and this it is which must inspire every true reformer of the church or the world. He must discover in divine truth "*the substance of things hoped for, the evidence of things not seen.*" And this is faith, the gospel faith, in its own integrity, simple yet powerful – simple, for a child can grasp it, and mighty enough to lay hold on God himself.

Is it not this which the disciples of the Lord in our own time need, in order to be "true and faithful witnesses" of God, and to carry on that great aggressive movement into the kingdom of darkness, which Jehovah declares is the mission of the church? "For this purpose have I raised thee up, to be my salvation to the ends of the earth. Behold, I send thee far hence to the Gentiles."

8
Family Matters – Chapels – Berridge

IN THE winter of 1756-57 Lady Huntingdon came to London with her family, and had her house opened twice a week for the preaching of the gospel, where Romaine and Venn principally officiated.

"I rejoice," says Whitefield, "in the increase of your ladyship's spiritual routs. I can guess at the consolation such scenes must give to your soul. No wonder you are distressed from other quarters. Indeed, my most noble and ever honoured patroness, thus it must be. Christ's witnesses must be purged at home. Inward domestic trials fit for outward public work. Nature recoils when constrained to take the cross, and it may be from a near and dear relation's hand; but infinite wisdom knows what is best."

The precise nature of these trials does not appear, unless we may take a hint of them from the Countess of Hertford, who exclaims,

"What an affliction is Lord Huntingdon's dislike to religion; and what have not my Lords Chesterfield and Bolingbroke to answer for. But he is most tender, respectful, and kind to Lady Huntingdon. This is some consolation, and may we not hope that in a course of time her example and the excellent instruction which he has received may have their full weight on his character?" She also adds, "He is a most interesting, elegant, and accomplished young nobleman, and very likely to make some figure in the world. He was much affected by the death of Miss Hotham, to whom it was said he was much attached."

Lady Gertrude Hotham, sister to Lady Chesterfield, has been already mentioned as one of the number who dared to be singular for the Lord's sake. Both in London and at Bath, she opened her house to the ministrations of Whitefield, and she had the happiness of seeing her eldest daughter born into the spiritual family of her Lord. Miss Hotham adorned her Christian profession both in her life and in her death, which took place in the bloom of a ripe and beautiful womanhood. While ill, many prayers were offered for her recovery at the administration of the Lord's Supper at Lady Huntingdon's, Lady Fanny Shirley's, and in her own home. One day when Whitefield came and knelt at her bedside, she was desired to remain as she was. "I can rise to take physic," she said; "why not to pray?" Her sick chamber bore the flowers and fruits of a thorough Christian experience. She knew whom she had believed, for the hope which she had in her Saviour was indeed like an anchor to her soul, sure and steadfast; and the peace and joy which she expressed even in the pangs of dying, served in a most affecting and striking manner to confirm, in the minds of her friends and worldly companions, the precious truths of that gospel which Whitefield proclaimed by his preaching.

Lady Elizabeth Hastings, Lady Huntingdon's eldest daughter, married the Earl of Moira, a branch of the Huntingdon family, and the connection seems to have given much satisfaction; but "Lady Selina," says one, "is the greatest comfort to her mother; she is a most pious, amiable, and affectionate character;" so that, if there were shadows on Lady Huntingdon's household, there were also sunbeams.

In September, 1757, we behold her suddenly called to Brighton by the illness of her fourth son, Honourable Henry Hastings, who died at the age of eighteen years.

"Oh what strong physics is our heavenly Father obliged to give us," wrote Whitefield to the bereaved mother. "What pruning-knives do these luxuriant branches require, in order to preserve the fruit and delicacy of the vine. Blessed be God, there is a time coming when these mysterious providences will be explained. May the Lord Jesus raise you up many comforters. Above all, may he come himself."

The Lord Jesus came himself, and so healing was his heavenly presence, that we find the mourner bearing the precious balm to the humble homes in her neighbourhood. Behold her at the obscure lodgings of a poor soldier's wife, carrying her food to eat and raiment to put on, and inviting her to "the Lamb of God, who taketh away the sin of the world." The woman's room was next to a public bakehouse, where the people who worked at the oven overheard the pious conversation of a lady through a crack in the ceiling. When her visits became known, other poor women begged to come in and be taught also, until a little company assembled daily with whom she prayed, read, and explained the Scriptures. One day a blacksmith, notorious for his wickedness, swore he would go to the meetings, and accordingly forced himself in behind the women. When Lady Huntingdon entered and saw a man in the corner, she was about to ask him to withdraw, but on second thought concluded to go on as usual. Her simple, direct, and affectionate exhortations touched the conscience of the bold blasphemer. He who came to scoff went away with the cry, "Lord, what shall I do to be saved?" A radical change took place in his character, and for nearly twenty-nine years he lived to adorn the doctrine of his Lord and Saviour.

One day as Lady Huntingdon was walking out, a lady suddenly accosted her, "Oh, madam, you are come." Surprised at so abrupt an address from an entire stranger, she feared the woman was deranged. "What do you know of me?" asked the countess. "Madam, I saw you in a dream three years ago, dressed as you now are," answered the stranger, and then related other circumstances connected with the dream. Singular as these circumstances were, an acquaintance was formed between them, and Lady Huntingdon became instrumental in the conversion of her new-found friend, who died a year afterwards in the triumphs of faith.

Thus did this remarkable woman lay out a field for the labours of Whitefield, who visited Brighton in 1759, and preached his first sermon under a spreading tree in the midst of a large meadow.

Brighton, or Brighthelmstone, as it was then commonly called, in the county of Sussex, fifty-two miles south of London, was not at that time the famous watering-place it has since become. Its buildings were comparatively mean and its population poor, presenting a strong contrast to the splendid edifices and spacious accommodations which now make Brighton one of the favourite summer resorts of the English.

A spirit of religious inquiry was kindled among the people. They hungered for the bread of life. Nor when they asked bread, could they be satisfied with a stone, or husks, for they wanted that of which if a man eat he shall never hunger. A small society gathered in an "upper chamber;" they were poor in worldly goods, but rich in faith; despised, but not forsaken. In order to strengthen their hands,

Lady Huntingdon determined to build a small chapel for their use near her own house in North Street, though straightened in means, for her benefactions were already numerous. To *resolve*, with her, was to *accomplish*. Wherein could she curtail? There lay her jewels, long since put aside for a pearl of infinitely greater price, and these she determined to offer to her Lord. They were sold for six hundred and ninety-eight pounds, and with this she erected a neat house of worship, which was opened in 1760. Here Romaine, Venn, and other godly men laboured with apostolic zeal, and though their work was often evil-spoken of, the Lord "added to the church daily such as should be saved." Brighton henceforth became one of her favourite places of residence. This was the small beginning of one of her greatest enterprises – this was the first of those houses of divine worship known by her name, which in a few years dotted the English soil; and its interests so prospered, that in five years the building needed a considerable enlargement.

On the day previous to its re-opening, she set apart several hours for private devotion, like Jacob of old, to wrestle with Jacob's God for his blessing on this sanctuary reared to his name; and in the evening a meeting was held at her house for the same purpose: so greatly did she honour the mercy-seat, and so firmly did she trust in the power of prayer.

At that time there were many spiritual wastes in the county of Sussex, and Lady Huntingdon was on the alert to cast in the good seed wherever an opportunity offered, or if possible to *make* opportunities in a cause so pressing and momentous. While making inquiries for securing a preaching spot at Oathall, ten miles from Brighton, an old gentleman unexpectedly came and offered to lease her for a certain number of years the mansion of Oathall, a house on an estate belonging to one branch of the Shirley family. His terms were promptly and thankfully accepted, and workmen were immediately engaged to fit up a large room for divine worship, and prepare the remainder of the house for the accommodation of herself and her chaplains. Here the gospel was faithfully preached, and with marked effect. During the summer, a regiment of soldiers was quartered in the vicinity. The captain, a carefree officer, went out one day on a sporting frolic, and was forced by a violent shower to seek shelter under a shed with a farmer and his labourers, with whom he soon entered into conversation; the farmer was a Christian man, and the talk took a religious turn. His remarks surprised and interested the officer, and he asked where so much had been learned about divine things.

"In that hall yonder," answered the farmer, "where there is a famous man, a Mr Romaine, preaching for Lady Huntingdon; you would do well to go and hear him for yourself."

Captain Scott, moved by all the circumstances, determined to do so, and on the following Sabbath bent his steps thitherward. On entering the hall, the devout and serious air of the congregation forcibly impressed his mind; while Mr Romaine's remarks from the words of the Saviour, "I am the way," were as goads and as nails fastened by the Master of assemblies upon his conscience.

Though a man of pleasure, there had been times when a profound seriousness came over him, compelling him to pause and ask, "Whither am I tending?" Nor had these seasons escaped the notice and ridicule of his companions. He was now in the presence of one who seemed to him to speak as man never before spoke, and they were truths just suited to his case. He afterwards made the acquaintance of Mr Romaine in London, whose prayers and instructions confirmed him in his resolutions to seek with all diligence to make his calling and election sure; and as he had proved himself a brave officer on the plains of Minden, so did he become valiant in a better service, even a heavenly.

When Captain Scott was on his way to Shropshire, Romaine gave him a letter for Mr Powys of Berwick, a gentleman of high connections and large fortune, and very zealous for the cause of God and truth. Venn was at that time paying him a visit. One morning after prayers, as they were looking from the hall window, Captain Scott rode onto the lawn mounted on his military charger and dressed in his uniform, bringing the letter entrusted to his care. Mr Powys recognised him in the distance and exclaimed, "There is Captain Scott. What can he want? How can I avoid seeing him?" for how great an interruption would a worldly officer be, with a guest like Venn of Huddersfield! The gentlemen withdrew. Scott rode up to the door, and was received with distant politeness by Mr Powys. On reading Romaine's letter, giving an account of the captain's conversion, Powys became much agitated; he ran to the officer, warmly embraced him, and cried out, "Mr Venn, Mrs Powys, come quickly. Here is Captain Scott, a convert to Christ; a new creature in Christ Jesus!" How great was their joy over him who had been lost, and was found; dead, and now made alive.

Let us hear of him again. "I went last Monday," said Fletcher, "to meet Captain Scott, one of the fruits that have grown for the Lord at Oathall – a captain of the truth – a bold soldier of Jesus Christ. God hath thrown down before him the middle wall of bigotry, and he boldly launches into an irregular usefulness. For some months he has exhorted his dragoons daily; for some weeks he has preached publicly at the Methodist meeting-house at Leicester, in his regimentals, to numerous congregations. The stiff ones pursue him with hue and cry, but I believe he is quite beyond their reach. God keep him zealous and simple. I believe this *red coat* will shame many a black one. I am sure he shames me."

Whitefield invited him to come to London and "bring his artillery to Tabernacle-rampart."

Captain Scott was an accomplished man, of an ancient and respectable family, with flattering prospects of worldly advancement; but worldly honours now ceased to charm him: he quitted the army for the ministry, and for twenty years was one of the supplies at the Tabernacle, and his new labours were crowned with abundant success. Another of the first-fruits of Oathall was an old man of a hundred years. He had long been serious, and had often complained that church-preaching was not like church-prayers; and though no friend to "new measures," old Abraham determined one day to go and hear for himself what kind of stuff they had at the chapel. He listened with the profoundest attention and delight while Mr Venn discoursed of the love of Christ, and could hardly contain himself for joy. "Ah, neighbour," he exclaimed, as soon as the services were over, tapping the shoulder of one who sat next to him, "this is the very truth of God's Word, which I have been for ever seeking, and never found before. Here will I tarry." And from that morning a new life was beating in the old man's bosom.

On one occasion when Brighton and Oathall were destitute of a supply, Lady Huntingdon sent for a distinguished revival preacher to spend a few weeks in these fields. In reply, he says, "I am determined not to quit my charge again in a hurry. Never do I leave my bees, though for a short space only, but on my return I find them either casting or colting, or fighting and robbing each other; not gathering honey from every flower of God's garden, but filling the air with their buzzings, and darting out the venom of their little hearts in their fiery stings. Nay, so inflamed they often are, and a mighty little thing disturbs them, that three months' tinkling after-wards with a warming-pan will scarce hive them at last, and make them settle to work again."

This quaint mixture of wit, sense, and bluntness came from *Rev John Berridge*, who is now introduced to our readers. His tall, stalwart figure looks as if it was made to wear; his deliberate and dis-tinct speech seems fit only for weighty words; but beneath the grave, nay, the solemn expression of his face there is lurking a quiet humour, which gives a genial warmth to his affections, and a gladsome play to his spirits, rarely found in the lonely life of a bachelor: yet it were a strange misnomer to call Berridge's life a lonely one, for it was as stirring as a hundred miles riding, with ten or twelve sermons a week, could make it, and that for a period of nearly five and twenty years. At home his table was ever ready for his hearers, many of whom came from a distance – his stables open to their horses; while houses and barns in every direction were rented and taken care of for the lay-preachers employed at his expense on errands of gospel love.

Berridge is settled at Everton, in Bedfordshire, about thirty miles north-west of London. In 1757, two years after his removal thither, he began to be in doubt and anxiety concerning his soul; for like many others he had entered upon the work of the ministry a stranger to that love which works by faith and purifies the heart. He beheld his own vineyard parched and dry, unvisited by those showers of mercy which enriched the labours of a more spiritual husbandry.

"Lord, direct me," was his importunate cry; "show me thy way, and lead me to a knowledge of the truth as it is in Jesus." The Holy Spirit visited his soul; a clearer light dawned upon his mind, and salvation by Christ became the corner-stone of his own hopes, and the refuge to which he bade all men flee from the wrath to come. The fruits of his new ministry he thus describes:

"Soon after I began to preach the gospel at Everton, the churches in the neighbourhood were deserted, and mine so overcrowded, that the squire, 'who did not like strangers,' he said, 'and hated to be incommoded,' joined with the offended parsons, and lodged a complaint against me. I was summoned before the bishop.

"'Well, Berridge,' said the bishop, 'did I institute you to Eaton, or Potten? why do you go preaching out of your parish?'

"'My lord,' says I, 'I make no claim to the living of those parishes; it is true I was once at Eaton, and finding a few poor people assembled, I admonished them to repent of their sins, and to believe in the Lord Jesus Christ for the salvation of their souls. At that very moment, my lord, there were five or six clergymen out of their own parishes, and enjoying themselves on the Eaton bowling-green.'

"'I tell you,' retorted his lordship, 'that if you continue preaching where you have no right, you will be very likely sent to Huntingdon jail.'

"'I have no more regard for a jail than other folks,' rejoined I, 'but I had rather go there with a good conscience than to be at liberty without one.'

"His lordship looked very hard at me. 'Poor fellow,' he said, 'you are beside yourself, and in a few months you will be either better or worse.'

"'Then, my lord,' said I, 'you may make yourself quite happy in this business; for if I should be better, you suppose I shall desist of my own accord, and if worse, you need not send me to Huntingdon jail, for I shall be better accommodated in Bedlam.'

"His lordship then pathetically entreated me, as one who had been and wished to continue my friend, not to embitter the remaining portion of his days by any squabbles with my brother clergymen, but to go home to my parish; and so long as I kept within it, I should be at liberty to do what I liked there. 'As to your conscience,' he said, 'you know that preaching out of your parish is contrary to the canons of the Church.'

"'There is one canon, my lord,' said I, 'which I dare not disobey, and that says, *Go preach the gospel to every creature.*'"

Although powerful patrons were displeased with Berridge's career, friends equally powerful were raised up for his defence, so that Everton and the region round about ever continued to enjoy the unstinted benefactions both of his heart and purse.

Berridge was forty in the year from which he dates his "new birth," 1757. A few months afterwards he met Wesley, and a little later Whitefield, against both of whom he had been strongly prejudiced. He now welcomed them as beloved brethren in the Lord. Lady Huntingdon soon made his acquaintance; a warm friendship sprang up between the two. Indeed, the richness and originality of his mind made him an especial favourite; while his sturdy sticking to his own notions of duty never gave offence to those who understood the depth and singleness of his piety.

9
The Valley of Baca

IN THE panoramic scene which now comes before us, we see Lady Huntingdon, in the beginning of 1757, at Bath, accompanied by Lady Fanny Shirley and her favourite daughter, Selina Hastings. On the fourth of January, she went to Bristol to meet Mr Wesley, who returned with her to Bath, and preached several times to the nobility at her house. Early in February she returns to London; and on a day of public fasting and prayer goes to the Tabernacle to hear Mr Whitefield, who addressed an immense audience from the solemn words, "Rend your hearts, and not your garments." In the evening she is at the Foundry, listening to Wesley, who preached to an overflowing multitude.

We now are present at the Lord's Supper, administered on a Tuesday at her own house, by Whitefield, assisted by Romaine and Madan. Of Whitefield's solemn address, she says, "All were touched to the heart, and dissolved in tears. My inmost soul felt penetrated by the height and depth of that love which passes knowledge, and I was ready to say with Peter, 'It is good to be here.' Lord, teach me how to improve to the utmost these gracious visitations."

Who the "all" were is not known, but among the communicants were the Countess of Chesterfield, Lady Gertrude Hotham, Earl and Countess of Dartmouth, Mr Thornton, Venn, Fletcher, and other less familiar names.

This service concluded, Earl Chesterfield, with a few others, entered, when Whitefield preached from the passage, "Him that cometh unto me I will in no wise cast out."

"The Lord was eminently present," she says; "the Word seemed clothed with an irresistible energy, and drew sighs from every heart, and tears from every eye. Mr Fletcher concluded with a prayer, every syllable of which seemed uttered under the immediate teachings of the Spirit; and he has told me since, that he never had more intimate communion with God, or enjoyed so much of his immediate presence, as on that occasion. Ah, how poor and trifling does all created good appear, when thus highly favoured of God. He in mercy keeps me sensible of my weakness and dependence upon himself, for which I praise him. He has strengthened my body to undergo more fatigue than usual, without being hurt by it. Bless the Lord, O my soul, and forget not all his benefits."

It was in the summer of this year that cries and convulsions, which attended the early preaching of Wesley, appeared among the hearers of Berridge. Lady Huntingdon begged Mr Romaine to visit Everton, and witness the phenomenon. He was warmly welcomed by the vicar and Mr Hicks of Westlingworth, whose preaching produced similar effects. After conversing with those who had fallen into convulsions, and accompanying the preachers on their rounds, he felt persuaded that the work was the religion of God, though occasionally mingled with the wildness of enthusiasm. Wesley also went to Everton for this purpose. "I have often observed," he tells us, "more or less of these outward symptoms to attend the beginning of a general work of God. So it was in New England, Scotland, Holland, Ireland, and many parts of England; but after a time they gradually decreased, and the work goes on more quietly and silently." Ralph Erskine treats the subject with less indulgence.

Wesley thus pleasantly discourses to Lady Huntingdon.

"The agreeable hour which I spent with your ladyship the last week, recalled to my mind the former times, and gave me much matter for thankfulness to the Giver of every good gift. I have found great satisfaction in conversing with those instruments whom God has lately raised up. But still there is, I know not what, in those whom we have known from the beginning, and who have borne the burden and heat of the day, which we do not find in those who have risen up since, though they are upright of heart. Perhaps, too, those who have lately come into the harvest are led to think and speak more largely of justification and the other first principles of the doctrine of Christ. And it may be proper for them to do so, yet *we* find a thirst after something further. We want to sink deeper and rise higher in the knowledge of God our Saviour. We want all helps for walking closely with him, whom we have received, that we may the more speedily come to the measure of the stature of the fulness of Christ.

"Mr Berridge appears to be one of the most simple, as well as most sensible men of all whom it pleases God to employ in reviving primitive Christianity. They come now twelve or fourteen miles to hear him, and very few come in vain. His word is with power; he speaks as plain and homely as John Nelson, but with all the propriety of Mr Romaine, and the tenderness of Mr Hervey.

"At Colchester, likewise, the Word has free course. On Sunday I was obliged to preach on St John's Green; the people stood on a smooth sloping ground, sheltered by the walls of an old castle, and behaved as men who felt that God was there.

"I am persuaded your ladyship still remembers in your prayers your willing servant, for Christ's sake,

"JOHN WESLEY"

Though Lady Huntingdon honoured and admired this noble reformer, he crosses the path of our narrative less frequently than we could wish. He occasionally preached both at her house and in her chapels, but his own field is broad, his own work great, and he is laying deep the foundations of that ecclesiastical polity which has given such expansive and conquering power to the Methodist connection.

Lady Huntingdon was anxious to visit Everton, and witness for herself the surprising effects produced there by the preaching of the gospel. On the morning after the arrival of her party, a large concourse of people assembled at an early hour. At seven o'clock, Mr Berridge preached in a field near the church, when the "power of God fell upon the assembled multitude in a very uncommon manner." Messrs. Venn, Madan, and Fletcher held services at other times of the day. The coming of Lady Huntingdon, and the preaching of her ministers, was speedily noised abroad, so that by the next day ten thousand assembled to hear them. While Mr Venn was impressively exhorting from the solemn words of the prophet, "The harvest is past, the summer is ended, and we are not saved," several individuals, men and women, "sank down and wept bitterly;" and in the evening, under the sharp, energetic eloquence of Berridge, "five persons, almost at once, sank down as dead;" others uttered, with a loud and bitter cry, "What must we do to be saved?" In a little time all was silent, and the preacher concluded his discourse.

On Lady Huntingdon's return to London, Berridge accompanied her, for she was anxious to introduce him into the religious circles of the metropolis. During his stay he preached several times in the city churches, assisted both Whitefield and Wesley, expounded almost every morning and evening at Park Street, besides occasional lectures at Lady Gertrude Hotham's, in Norfolk Street, Grosvenor Square, and Lady Fanny Shirley's in South Audley Street.

Favoured as Oak Hall had been by the blessing of God, it was here that Lady Huntingdon was visited by one of her severest family afflictions, which was the death by fever of her youngest born, Lady Selina Hastings, at the age of twenty-six.

Amiable, accomplished, and devotedly attached to her mother, Lady Huntingdon's cares were lightened by her true affection and sympathy.

She was one of the six earl's daughters chosen to assist the Princess Augusta to bear the train of Queen Charlotte on her coronation day; and she was soon to have been married to Colonel George Hastings, a connection much approved by her mother. And yet these charms of the present life had not rendered her unmindful of that life which is to come.

"She was my dearest," said the weeping mother, "the desire of my eyes, and the continual pleasure of my heart."

"On her going to bed the day she was taken ill," continues she, from whose lips we will learn of the last sad scenes, "she said she should never rise from it more. She said she did not begin to think about death then, and that she had no desire to live; 'Therefore, my dear mother, why not now? The Lord can make me ready any moment; and if I live longer, I may not be better prepared.' She desired me to pray by her, and with great earnestness accompanied me. At one time she called me, and said, 'My dearest mother, come and lie down by me, and let my heart be laid close to yours, and then I shall get rest.'

"During the last four days, she often exclaimed, 'Jesus, teach me; Jesus, cleanse me; Jesus, wash me.' The day before her death, I came to her, and asked if she knew me. 'My dearest mother,' she answered. I asked her if she were happy. Raising her head from the pillow, she whispered, 'I am happy, very, *very* happy;' and then put out her lips to kiss me. She gave directions to her servant, Catharine Spooner, about the disposal of some rings; observing, that she mentioned it to her, lest it should shock her dear mother to tell her. She often said, 'To be resigned to God's will was all, and that she had no hope of salvation but in the mercy of Jesus Christ.' Blessed are the dead who die in the Lord."

Letters of sympathy and consolation came in from all her friends. Those of Mr Berridge are worthy of many readings.

"My Lady – I received your letter from Brighthelmstone, and hope you will soon learn to bless your Redeemer for snatching away your daughter so speedily. Methinks I see great mercy in the suddenness of her removal; and when your bowels have done yearning for her, you will see it too. Oh, what is she snatched from? Why, truly from the plague of an evil heart, a wicked world, and a crafty devil – snatched from all such bitter grief as now overwhelms you – snatched from everything that might wound her ear, afflict her eye, or pain her heart. And what is she snatched to? To a land of everlasting peace, where the voice of the turtle is ever heard, where every inhabitant can ever say, 'I am no more sick:' no more whim in the head, no more plague in the heart, but all full of love and full of praise; ever seeing with enraptured eyes, ever blessing with adoring hearts, that dear Lamb who has washed them in his blood, and has now made them kings and priests unto God for ever and ever, Amen.

"Oh, madam, what would you have? Is it not better to sing in heaven, 'Worthy is the Lamb, that was slain,' than to be crying at Oathall, 'O wretched woman that I am?' Is it not better for her to go before, than to stay after you? and then to be lamenting, 'Ah, my mother!' as you now lament, 'Ah, my daughter!' Is it not better to have your Selina taken to heaven, than to have your heart divided between Christ and Selina? If she was a silver idol before, might she not have proved a golden one afterwards? She has gone to pay a most blessed visit, and you will see her again, never to part more. Had she crossed the sea, and gone to Ireland, you could have borne it; but now she has gone to heaven, it is almost intolerable.

"Wonderful, strange love is this! Such behaviour in others would not surprise me, but I could almost beat you for it; and I am sure

Selina would too, if she was called back but for one moment from heaven to gratify your fond desires. I cannot soothe you, and I must not flatter you. I am glad the dear creature has gone to heaven before you. Lament if you please, but glory, glory, glory be to God, says,

"JOHN BERRIDGE."

In another letter, a week later, he says, "Oh, heart, heart, what art thou? a mess of fooleries and absurdities; the vainest, foolishest, craftiest, wickedest thing in nature. And yet the Lord Jesus asks me for this heart, woos me for it, died to win it! O, wonderful love; adorable condescension!

"Take it, Lord, and let it be
Ever closed to all but thee."

A fortnight later, he again says, "Mrs Bateman has sent me a mighty pretty letter to coax me into Sussex, and withal acquaints me that your ladyship has been ill of a fever, and is now better. I was glad to hear of both. Nothing expels undue grief of mind like bodily corrections. Nothing makes the child leave crying like the rod; at least, I find it so by experience. However, I durst not send such consolations to many Christians, because they are not able to see the truth, or bear the weight of it. I found your heart was sorely pained, and I pitied you, but I durst not soothe you; for soothing, though it eases grief but a moment, only makes Lady Self more burdensome, and occasions more tears in the end. A little whipping from your Father will dry up your tears much sooner than a thousand pretty lullabies from your brethren. I now hope you will be well soon."

Venn tenderly writes from Huddersfield, "Among the many in these parts who have a love for your ladyship's name, and a tender sympathy with you as a member of Christ, I desire to assure your ladyship, I do not forget to offer up many prayers that your present very severe cross may be sanctified, and the agonising separation made supportable by larger manifestations of the faithfulness and marvellous loving-kindness of God our Saviour."

As soon as it was possible for him to leave his charge, Venn visited the bereaved mother at Brighton, and went back from there to London to superintend the publication of his "*Complete Duty of Man*," which was brought out during this year, 1763. Precious as his visit must have been to the mourner, he could respond, "It was indeed a great blessing to my soul;" so unspeakably enriching is that fellowship which is in Christ Jesus.

Berridge also came to Oathall during the summer, where his ministrations were cordially welcomed by the people in all the region round about. Whitefield was on his way to the New World.

Grimshaw of Haworth also died in the spring of this year, of a highly infectious fever, which spread extensively through his parish. From the first attack of the disease he felt that it would be fatal, and looked in the face of the king of terrors as if it had been the face of an angel. "Never had I such a visit from God since I knew him," said the dying man. He was in the fifty-fifth year of his age, and the twenty-first of his ministry at Haworth.

10

Blackfriars – Chapel at Bath – Lady Glenorchy

FOR many years Mr Romaine lived in Walnut Tree Walk, Lambeth, where he had a little garden, which he planted and took care of himself; and where, with his annuals and biennials, sprung up also immortal plants, for in 1755 he married, and children were born to him. His regular salary at this time was but eighteen pounds a year, derived from the lectureship of St Dunstan's; and though the means of living flowed in from other sources, he was compelled to be frugal in his habits, and prudent in his expenditures. Equally frugal of his time, he often received his friends to an early breakfast. "I breakfasted one morning with him," said a young clergyman, "and on taking some bread, which I thought very good, he spoke of a certain physician who thought London bread should not be given to sick people, on account of its too frequent adulteration previous to baking: he then clearly and forcibly touched on a variety of modes by which the Word of God was mixed up with the ill-leaven of other ingredients, so as to deprive it of its heaven-imparted sustenance; and this he did in such easy, familiar, and yet pointed terms, and with such paternal benignity of look, that I was equally pleased and profited by the interview, and it has certainly served to render bread to me of more value, both as a support and as a sign." Thus was he intent upon turning every occasion to some spiritual account.

In 1764, the living of St Ann's, Blackfriars, became vacant, "and it was immediately impressed upon my mind, that the vacancy was to be filled by dear Mr Romaine," said Lady Huntingdon, opening the matter to the Lord Chancellor. The right of presentation was vested alternately in the crown and in the parishioners; it was now subject to the latter. The parishioners were sounded by his friends, and although some of them had entertained little hopes of his success, to their surprise there was a general interest in his favour. "But he is too proud to ask your votes," it was said by his opponents, "while the candidate in canonicals comes hat in hand, bowing from door to door." Mr Romaine, who was absent in Yorkshire, was speedily apprised of what his friends had been doing on his behalf; and at the time appointed for the candidates to preach, he was in London, and preached from the words, "We preach not ourselves, but Christ Jesus the Lord, and ourselves your servants for Jesus' sake."

Alluding to the reports which had been circulated in consequence of his not having solicited their votes in the too common way, he says, "Some have insinuated it was from pride that I would not go about the parish, from house to house, canvassing for votes; but truly it was another motive. I could not see how this could promote the glory of God. How can it be for the honour of Jesus, that his ministers, who have renounced fame and riches and ease, should be most anxious and earnest in the pursuit of those very things which they have renounced? Surely this would be getting into a worldly spirit, as much as the spirit of parliamenteering. And as this method of canvassing cannot be for Jesus' sake, neither can it be for his honour: it is far beneath our function; nor is it for your profit. What good is it to your souls? What compliment to your understandings? Is it not depriving you of the freedom of your choice? Determined by these motives, when my friends of their own accord put me up as a candidate, to whom I have to this hour made no application, directly or indirectly, I left you to yourselves. If you choose me, I desire to be your servant for Jesus' sake; and if you do not, the will of the Lord be done."

This dignified stand won him favour: at the second balloting, Mr Romaine received a large majority of votes; but the two other candidates taking advantage of some flaw in the manner of proceeding, the case was carried into the court of Chancery. It was some time before the matter was decided, and Romaine was accused of being too easy about the result. "Blackfriars church is desirable," he replies, "but we cannot tell whether Jesus wants it or not: if he does, he will bring it about; if not, his will be done."

While this important matter was pending, we find Lady Huntingdon and her chaplains sowing and reaping at Lewes, situated at the edge of the South Downs, eight miles north-east of Brighton. The town is ancient and of marked historical interest. In the ivy-clad ruins of a castle and priory are the memorials of a feudal age, of monks and cowls; here also was a battleground once red with the conflict between royal and baronial power; "the Mise of Lewes" is known in history as one of those agreements which armed men entered upon only to break at a more convenient season. Lady Huntingdon obtained one of the regular churches for Mr Romaine; his searching appeals angered his brethren, and he was refused another hearing: a large room was then obtained, and, better still, such was the irrepressible eagerness with which the people flocked to hear him, he spoke in the open air. "All gave solemn heed," said Lady Huntingdon, "while he applied those solemn words, 'Behold the Lamb of God, who taketh away the sin of the world.' I did not see one careless or inattentive person, and there is reason to think many poor sinners were cut to the heart."

In the same year also, 1765, active measures were taken to erect a chapel at Bath, the resort alike of the fashionable and the afflicted. The summer months found this city thronged with people in quest of change, excitement, society, or health, – thoughtless, restless, aimless.

From time to time, Whitefield had proclaimed here the "good tidings" of redemption. As early as 1752 he preached at the house of Lady Huntingdon for three weeks to large circles of the carefree world; three years afterwards, Lady Gertrude Hotham threw open her doors for his ministrations; the city had also been blessed in less public ways with the labours of those who loved their Lord; and it seemed to be now a fitting time for the creation of a place of worship where the awakened clergy could have a wider sphere to work in.

In the summer of 1765, Lady Huntingdon bought a piece of land in the vineyards of Bath, and made preparations for building. Meanwhile Lord Chesterfield offered his chapel at Bretly Hall, in Derbyshire, to be used by her chaplains during their summer tours. Gladly did she accept the offer; and the old domain, so often echoing with the noise of revelry, now resounded with the proclamations of the gospel, for Romaine is in the pulpit, and Whitefield in the park. This was in July. Referring to this period, Romaine says, "Fifteen pulpits were open to me here, and showers of grace came down."

One of the gentlemen of Lady Huntingdon's party rambled one day among the grand and beautiful scenes of the famous Derbyshire peaks. Weary with his wanderings, he sought rest and refreshment in a humble cottage among the heights. Beginning a talk with the woman, he was surprised to find her an intelligent and warm-hearted Christian. He asked if there were many like-minded, and if the gospel were often preached in her neighbourhood.

"Alas, no," she replied, "I have not a creature of the same mind to converse with; I am quite alone; those I see and talk with know nothing of the grace of God in Christ."

"And pray, how came you to know it?" asked the gentleman.

"Why sir," she answered, "some time ago there was a famous man down in this country, called Mr Romaine; he preached some miles off, and many of the neighbours went to hear him. So I thought I would go too; accordingly away I trudged, and he had no sooner begun his discourse, than it all seemed directed to me: he opened the depravity of my heart, convinced my conscience of my sins, showed me the wages of death which were due to me, and the truth of it I felt in my own soul. He then opened the fulness and glory of Christ, described his sufferings and death, displayed the riches of his grace to the miserable, and invited them to embrace it and be blessed. Sir, you cannot think the instantaneous and wonderful effect it had on me; I was convinced of sin, justified by faith, and came home rejoicing. From that day to this I have never lost the sweet savour of those truths. How I long to see the gentleman again. Do you know him? I think they said he came from London."

The gentleman and the poor cottager were no longer strangers. They were of the same spiritual household, and beheld in each other the likeness of their Lord. She had probably heard the London preacher on one of his summer tours to Ashby, which was not far off.

By October, the chapel at Bath was finished. In the latter part of September, Lady Huntingdon sent for Romaine to attend her at Bath. He is now in Brighton, and replies, "The society most earnestly entreat you, if Mr Madan should come down to Bath, that I may be suffered to stay here with them. Why should Bath have all, and poor Brighton none? My very heart and soul are at work here now, inasmuch as I have not minded going to Oathall wet to the skin, for the joy that was set before me." Lady Huntingdon urged no more. On the 6th of October, the dedication services were performed by Whitefield, who says, "Though a wet day, the place was crowded; and assuredly the great Shepherd and Bishop of souls consecrated and made it holy ground by his presence."

Here Romaine spent many of his vacations; and though he had not the commanding eloquence of Whitefield, his clear and pungent exhibitions of truth, sharpened by a critical knowledge of the Word of God, powerfully affected the consciences of his hearers, and constrained men to flee from the wrath to come. Here also Fletcher pleaded with the prodigals and prayerless, with that irresistible sweetness and seriousness so peculiar to him. "Dear Mr Fletcher's preaching is truly apostolic," says Lady Huntingdon; "the divine blessing accompanies his preaching in a very remarkable manner; he is ever at his work, is amazingly followed, and singularly owned of God."

The chapel was not only frequented by the true hearers of God's Word, but the fame of its eloquent preachers attracted the most distinguished visitors of Bath. "It is certainly very neat, with its true Gothic windows," Horace Walpole tells us, who went there to hear Wesley; "I was glad to see luxury creeping in upon them before persecution. They have boys and girls with charming voices, who sing hymns in parts. At the upper end is a broad hautpas of four steps advancing in the middle; at each end of the broadest part are two eagles, with red cushions for the parson and clerk. Behind them rise three more steps, in the midst of which is a third eagle for a pulpit; scarlet armchairs in all three. The congregation sit on forms. Wesley is a clean elderly man, fresh coloured, his hair smoothly combed, but with a little soupçon of curls at the ends. Wondrous clever, but as evidently an actor as Garrick. There were parts and eloquence in his sermon, but towards the end he exalted his voice and acted very vulgar enthusiasm."

"Many were not a little surprised at seeing me in the Countess of Huntingdon's chapel," says Wesley; "the congregation was not only large, but serious, and I fully delivered my soul."

Among the visitors of Bath this season, were Lord and Lady Glenorchy of Scotland. They had just returned from the gaieties and excitement of a continental tour, when Lady Glenorchy was laid by from a severe illness at Great Sugnal, situated a short distance from Hawkstone, the celebrated seat of Sir Rowland Hill. Lady Glenorchy's intimacy with the Hill family had led her to some acquaintance with a spiritual Christianity, and impressed strongly upon her mind the idea that there was a higher and better life than that of a heartless round of fashionable follies. On her sick-bed that life dawned upon her soul. She found Jesus Christ, the tried corner-stone, elect and precious; and though gifted, beautiful, and young, for she was now but twenty-four, Lady Glenorchy resolutely turned her back upon the world, and consecrated herself to the service of her heavenly Master. Her nearest friends were alarmed and angry; they hastened to drive from her mind this strange and unwonted seriousness, and her husband was advised immediately to leave the country for the more lively resorts of Bath and London. They came to Bath: at Bath she met Lady Huntingdon, and at Bath she had a precious opportunity of hearing that preaching which confirmed her faith and nourished her soul. She was one of the earliest attendants upon the ministrations of the new chapel.

"Doubtless the world condemns your choice," wrote Miss Hill, almost the only pious friend whose instruction and countenance Lady Glenorchy enjoyed, "and has been telling you, you are sadly lost to your friends and acquaintances, and with an affected sort of pity would fain entangle you in its snares. 'Remember,' saith our blessed Lord, 'the word that I said unto you, The servant is not greater than his Lord: if they have persecuted me, they will also persecute you; if they have kept my saying, they will keep yours also. These things have I spoken unto you, that ye should not be offended.' These words of our Lord are sufficient consolation to every believer. Under their influence let us, my dear friend, learn daily that glorious lesson, to 'count all things but loss for the excellency of the knowledge of Christ Jesus our Lord,' and think it our highest honour, that as we can *do* so little for Christ, we should be called in some way or other to *suffer* for him, till he gives us our discharge and takes us to share the triumphs of that victorious faith which overcometh the world. May this be our happy lot.

"I rejoice that you had resolution and fortitude to resist all places of public amusement at Bath, and that you were enabled to see the vast danger you were in of being again entangled in the world; whose delights you now happily find to be so truly empty and so greatly disproportionate to the moral capacities of the soul, that they are no more capable of yielding any solid contentment to an immortal mind, than the glow-worm glistening in the hedge is capable of giving light to the universe. Let us remember, that whatever we make our chief delight, to the neglect of Christ and his salvation, as it is vanity in the fruition, so it shall surely be bitterness in the end. But if the blessed Jesus say to us, 'Be of good cheer, your sins are forgiven you,' and add that blessed promise, 'I will never leave you, nor forsake you,' we cannot but be truly happy. Let me warn you not to give way to unbelieving doubts and fears, which are highly dishonourable to God, and most destructive to your own peace and comfort. *Do trust him;* he will certainly perfect the work he has begun. What if your duties are imperfect, your graces at times weak, and your comforts fail; is not Christ still the same? Look upon him as a *full* Saviour, and rest satisfied that he can save to the uttermost."

Lady Huntingdon became deeply interested in this youthful disciple, thus struggling with foes within and temptations without, and we may well suppose how comforting and inspiring both her conversation and example must have been to the fainting, yet faithful heart of Lady Glenorchy.

On her return to Edinburgh in the spring, we find her not unmindful of the blessing, for she writes, "How shall I express the sense I have of your goodness, my dear madam? It is impossible, in words. When you say your heart is attached to me, I tremble lest I prove an additional cross to you in the end, and the pain I suffer in the apprehension of this is unspeakable. I hope the Lord permits it as a spur to me to be watchful, and to keep near to him, who alone is able to keep me from falling. I can truly say, that next to the favour of God, my utmost ambition is to be found worthy of the regard which your ladyship is pleased to honour me with, and to be one of those who shall make up the crown of your rejoicing in the day of our Lord."

Soon after her departure, arrived Lady Sutherland, sister of Lady Glenorchy, accompanied by her husband, both of whom were deeply suffering from the death of their eldest born. They were commended to Lady Huntingdon's ever ready sympathies. "Never," says she, "have I seen a more lovely couple; they may indeed with justice be called the Flower of Scotland. The good providence of God has, I hope, directed them here in order to lead them to the fountain of living waters. Dear Lady Glenorchy is extremely anxious on their account."

They attended the preaching of Whitefield, who was then at Bath; but only for a little while, for both, within a short time of each other, died of putrid-fever. The mournful event spread a general gloom over the bright city, and for a moment there seemed to be a pause in the whirl of pleasure. Two sermons were preached on the occasion in Lady Huntingdon's chapel, attended by almost all the nobility then at Bath.

During the summer, Whitefield spent much time between Bath and Bristol. "As my feverish heat continues," he says, "and the weather is too wet to travel, I have complied with the advice of friends, and commenced hot-well-water drinking twice a day. However, twice this week, at six in the morning, I have been enabled to call thirsty souls to come and drink of the water of life freely. Tomorrow evening, God-willing, the call is to be repeated. Good seasons at Bath; good seasons at Bristol. Large auditories. Grace, grace."

Whitefield was followed by Venn, who not only instructed and inspired from the pulpit, but charmed by the easy flow of his conversation in the social circle.

To return to St Ann's, Blackfriars, and the suit between Romaine and his competitors pending in Chancery. In February, 1766, a decree was issued in his favour, to the great joy of all who knew him and felt for the cause of truth. While receiving the congratulations of his friends, he simply said with profound seriousness, "It is my Master's will, and I submit."

To Lady Huntingdon he writes, "I had promised myself a little rest and retirement in the evening of life, but my fine plan is broken all to pieces. I am called into a public station and to the sharpest engagement, just as I had got into winter quarters – an engagement for life. I can see nothing before me, so long as I live, but war, and that with unreasonable men, a divided parish, an angry clergy, a wicked Sodom, and a wicked world; all to be resisted and overcome. Besides all these, a sworn enemy, subtle and cruel, with whom I can make no peace, no, not a moment's truce, night and day, with all his children and his host, is aiming at my destruction.

"When I take counsel of the flesh, I begin to faint; but when I go to the sanctuary, I see my cause good, and my Master is almighty, a tried friend; and then he makes my courage revive. Although I am no way fit for the work, yet he called me to it, and on him I depend for strength to do it, and for success to crown it. I utterly despair of doing anything as of myself, and therefore the more I have to do,

I shall be forced to live more by faith upon him. In this view, I hope to get *a great income by my living;* I shall want my Jesus more, and shall get closer to him. As he has made my application to him more necessary and more constant, he has given me stronger tokens of his love. Methinks I can hear his sweet voice, 'Come closer, come closer, soul; nearer yet: I will bring you into circumstances that you cannot do one moment without me.'"

Romaine was now fifty years of age, beginning a new career of thirty years' labour.

11

The Indian Preacher – Dartmouth – Lord Buchan

THE red men who roamed through the dense forests skirting their American colonies, were objects of intense and curious interest to the people of England. While stories of wild adventure and romantic incident "lent enchantment" to these far-off regions, the darkness and degradation of savage life pressed sorrowfully upon the Christian heart; efforts made to propagate the gospel among the tribes were cordially responded to by English Christians; and when *Samson Occum*, an Indian preacher, visited those eastern shores and stood before a London audience, he was welcomed as the first-fruits of a speedy and glorious harvest.

Dr Wheelock's school for the education of Indian youth, at Lebanon, Connecticut, excited a general interest. It was patronised by the chief men of the colonies, and besides other generous contributions both at home and from abroad, Mr Joshua Moor, a farmer of Mansfield, Connecticut, had made it a substantial gift of land, with a building for a school-house; in memory of which, the school was called Moor's Indian Charity school. Whitefield took it by the hand and commended it to the kind charities of his English friends.

"My very dear Dr Wheelock," he writes from London in 1760, "I have just time to write to you, that upon mentioning and a little enforcing your Indian affair, the Lord of all lords put it into the heart of the Marquis of Lothian to put into my hands fifty pounds sterling; you will not fail to send his lordship a letter of thanks and some account of the school. Now the great God has given us Canada, what will become of us, if we do not improve it to his glory and the conversion of the poor heathen? Satan is doing what he can here to bring the work into contempt, by blasphemy and ridicule from both theatres. But you know how the bush burned and was not consumed; and why? Jesus was, and is in it; Hallelujah. My hearty love to the Indian lambs."

A hundred pounds came also from an unknown lady; who she was, with Dr Wheelock, we may be permitted to conjecture. The doctor thus replies to a friendly and encouraging letter from Lady Huntingdon. "It animates and refreshes me much to find such fervent love to Christ, and earnest care for the perishing souls of poor savages, breathed forth by a lady of such distinction. My Indian school lives and flourishes only by the grace of God. My number of late has been twenty-six. Two young English gentlemen belonging to it were lately ordained to the sacred work, with a view, as soon as provision can be made for their support, to a mission among the Six nations. Three young Indians are appointed to be schoolmasters among those tribes, and six more to be assistants for the summer, and return here in the fall. The aforesaid youth, were all appointed to their respective services, not knowing we had a penny in stock to support them, till a few days ago we were informed by Mr Whitefield's letter of a hundred pounds sterling from a lady unknown, devoted to the service of this Indian design. My soul blesses the benefactress, and the blessing of many ready to perish, I trust, will come upon her. And then we, who can only conjecture by whom the favour is conferred, shall, by the account itself, and by the crown of glory given as the reward of it, be fully assured of the hand by whom it was done, where there shall be neither a possibility or occasion to conceal her liberality any more."

The expenses of the school still outrunning its ordinary supplies, Dr Wheelock, with the advice of his friends, concluded to send Samson Occum, one of the most promising of his graduates, and then preacher among the Narragansetts, in company with Rev Nathaniel Whitaker of Norwich, to solicit benefactions in England. They arrived in England in the summer of 1767.

Having brought letters of introduction to Lady Huntingdon, and already enjoying the personal friendship of Whitefield, who was then in his native land, they were speedily introduced into the religious circles of the metropolis. Occum excited universal attention. He preached to large audiences both at the Tabernacle and Tottingham chapel; and in his journey through England and Scotland, was warmly welcomed by Christians of every name.

"May God mercifully preserve him from the snares of the devil," ejaculated his old instructor on hearing of his flattering reception in the Old World.

As the fruit of missionary enterprise and a specimen of well-directed efforts to Christianise the savages, the presence of Occum not only encouraged Christian benevolence, but shamed the lukewarm and silenced the heartless ridicule of opposers. Whitefield, Wesley, Romaine, and Venn, all advocated the school, and money flowed generously in. A board of trustees was organised in London to receive contributions and disburse them to Dr Wheelock, according to his needs. The Earl of Dartmouth was chosen as president of this board, among whom we find the well-known names of Charles Hotham and John Thornton. Seven thousand pounds were collected in England, and between two and three thousand in Scotland; and thus, through the favour of God, the interests of this little school found lodgement in the hearts of the great and good.

As its course of study was limited, and its pupils had to be sent to distant colleges in order to complete their preparations for future usefulness, it was now thought advisable by its friends in the colonies, to enlarge its sphere of operations by removing it to a more eligible location and connecting a college with it. Generous offers were made by different and distant towns, to have it located within their borders. General Lyman was anxious it should come within his grant of government land on the Mississippi. The governor of Massachusetts offered it a large tract in Berkshire county; a larger offer was made by the city of Albany, and a still more generous one issued from Governor Wentworth of New Hampshire, consisting of five hundred acres of land in the township of Hanover, and a charter of the township of Llandaff, consisting of twenty-four thousand acres, with his own agency to procure a royal charter for the college.

Dr Wheelock sent these different proposals to the Earl of Dartmouth, asking the advice of the board of trustees. The offer of Governor Wentworth was accepted, and the little shoot was planted in a *granite soil.*

It was in August, 1770, that Dr Wheelock, then in his sixty-first year, went forth from the ease and comfort of the older settlements to make a new home in the yet unbroken forests. The lofty pines were levelled, a little clearing opened to the sunlight, and a few rude cabins erected, when the doctor's family and pupils, numbering seventy persons, began their toilsome journey to the north. The ladies lumbered along in a coach given him by some London friends; the rest, on horseback and on foot, left the travelled roads and plunged into the rude paths of the wood; the journey occupying as many weeks then, as it now does hours. The doctor, like a patriarch in the desert, gave them a hearty welcome in the name of the Lord: gathering his flock around him, a hymn of praise and the voice of grateful prayer broke upon the deep solitudes of the wilderness. His cheerful courage and unflinching faith inspired the most desponding; while, with the activity and enterprise of youth, he laid out plans, selected sites, and shared all the privations of his fellow-workers.

The frame of a college building, eighty feet in length and two stories in height, was soon raised and partially covered; a hall and two or three rooms were nearly finished, when the autumn storms, coming on earlier than usual, put a stop to further progress. Many were the hardships of this little colony during the first year of its existence; want of water, scanty supplies, coarse fare, drifting snows, beds made of boughs, with the nameless, yet numerous discomforts of new settlers, made up the stern discipline of this long and dreary winter. Like Elijah, who founded a school of the prophets in the wilderness of Jordan, the good man fainted not, but trusted in Him who is the refuge and the fortress of his people. Though the snow lay four feet deep, and the sun was long in climbing above the topmost pine – though the cold north-wester came like the breath of icebergs, there were warm hearts and devout spirits and busy hands in this forest clearing.

God too was there with the tokens of his favour. Through the reviving and converting influences of his grace, Dr Wheelock, in January, had the unspeakable satisfaction of gathering from his flock a church of thirty members, who made a solemn dedication of themselves to the service of God.

As a testimony of respect to William Earl of Dartmouth, one of its earliest patrons and benefactors, this institution was named Dartmouth College; and expressive of its birth and aim, its seal bears the significant motto, "*Vox clamantis in deserto*" – "The voice of one crying in the wilderness." Dartmouth College, in the town of Hanover, New Hampshire, is the cherished and venerated alma mater of many great and good men, whose names live in the great heart of the republic, and whose virtues are the treasures of the church.

A portrait of its patron hangs in one of the college halls. We look with admiration upon the handsome features and ripened manhood of this wealthy and accomplished English peer, but better and more beautiful still is it to think of him as casting all his honours at the Saviour's feet, and counting it his highest privilege to be known as a follower of Christ.

The king and some noblemen were once going out upon an early morning ride. Waiting a few moments for Lord Dartmouth, one of the party rebuked him for his tardiness. "I have learned to wait upon the King of kings before I wait on my earthly sovereign," was his reply. May the lofty and uncompromising tone of his religious character ever distinguish the institution which bears his name.

The same year that Occum visited England, and made glad the heart of Lady Huntingdon, she sorrowed over the death of a dear and valued friend, Mrs Venn, who died at Huddersfield in the autumn of 1767. To sound judgment and exalted piety, there was added a sweetness and vivacity of manner which rendered Mrs Venn a charming companion. A friendship sprang up between the two on their first introduction, while the Venns lived at Clapham, and it ever continued a source of profit and pleasure to both. Mr Venn was deeply bereaved by the death of his wife; it was an "unspeakable loss" both to himself and his children, yet behold the consolations vouchsafed to the children of God when afflictions break in like a flood.

"Since the moment she left me," wrote the weeping husband to Lady Huntingdon, "I can compare my sense of her being with the Lord to nothing but a vision, it is so clear, so constant, so delightful. At the same time the Lord gives me to see his own infinite beauty, and to feel more and more his preciousness as a fountain of living waters to those who are bereft of earthly joy. And well it is I am so supported. For his own cause I cannot but conclude the Lord does it, since immediately upon my unspeakable loss the opposers cried out, 'Oh, now you will see what will become of his vauntings of the power of faith, and the name of Jesus.' They knew our great happiness, and they said, 'You will see your vicar just like any one of us in the same situation.' But my God heard and answered; so that when I was mightily helped by him to preach the very Sabbath after her death, and not many hours after her interment, their mouths were stopped, and the little flock of Jesus, who had been praying for me with all fervour and affection, say they have not had so great a blessing since I have been among them."

The death also of Lord Buchan, a Scottish peer, with the solemn pomp which attended his burial, made a pause in the gaieties of Bath, and plunged into sorrow a family circle whom Lady Huntingdon dearly prized. He was brother to Lady Frances Gardiner, and had long been intimately associated with the religious circles of Scotland. In quest of health, he came with his family to Bath just after the opening of the Bath chapel; here his intimacy was renewed with Lady Huntingdon, and his family was favoured with frequent intercourse with all the awakening preachers of the day.

Lord Buchan found no alleviation of his malady; his health grew worse, but with the daily increasing feebleness of his body, his soul was renewed day by day. From the means of grace, to which he gave diligent heed, and the conversation of many eminent Christians, he gained clear views of Bible truth, and was enabled to lay hold of the doctrines of the cross as he had never done before. A few days before his death, he sent for Lady Huntingdon to visit him. Grasping her hand, he exclaimed, "I have no foundation of hope whatever, but in the sacrifice of the Son of God; I have nowhere else to look, nothing else to depend upon for eternal life and salvation, and my confidence in him is firm as a rock."

The impressive services which took place at his funeral are so different from anything within the range of our observation in America, that we may perhaps like to hear Whitefield's account of them. "All hath been awful, and more than awful," he tells us. "On Saturday evening, before the corpse was taken from Buchan house, a word of exhortation, and a hymn sung in the room where the corpse lay. The young earl stood with his hand on the head of the coffin, the countess dowager on his right hand, Lady Anne and Lady Isabella on his left, with other relatives on one side; a few friends, with all the domestics, on the other. At ten, the corpse was removed to good Lady Huntingdon's chapel, where it was deposited within a space railed, covered with black baize and the usual funeral concomitants, except the escutcheons. On Sunday morning all attended in mourning at early sacrament. They were seated by themselves at the foot of the corpse, and, with their head servants, received first, and a particular address was made to them. Immediately after receiving, these verses were sung for them:

"'Our lives, our blood we here present,
If for thy truths they may be spent;
Fulfil thy sovereign counsel, Lord,
Thy will be done, thy name adored.

Give them thy strength, O God of power,
And then, though men and devils roar,
Thy faithful witnesses they'll be:
'Tis fixed they can do all through thee.'

"Then they received the blessing, and the noble mourners returned to the good Lady Huntingdon's house, which was lent them for the day. At eleven, public services began. The bereaved relatives sat in order within, and the servants outside the rail. The chapel was more than crowded; near three hundred tickets, signed by the present earl, were given out to the nobility and gentry to be admitted. All was hushed and solemn. Proper hymns were sung, and I preached from these words: 'I heard a voice from heaven, saying unto me, Write, Blessed are the dead that die in the Lord.' Deep and almost universal impressions were made. The like scene, and, if possible, more solemn, was exhibited in the evening. Ever since, there hath been public service and preaching twice a day. This is to be continued till Friday morning; then all is to be removed to Bristol, in order to be shipped to Scotland. For five days together we have been attending to the house of mourning. Many, I trust, are obliged to say, 'How dreadful is this place.' Such a scene I never expect to see opened again this side of eternity. Surely the death of this noble earl will prove the life of many. He had great foretastes of heaven: he cried, 'Come, Holy Ghost.' He came, and filled him with great joy. 'Happy! happy!' were his last words. The survivors feel the influence; they sit round the corpse, attended by their domestics and supporters, twice a day. Two sermons every day."

The young earl, twenty-four years of age at his father's death, joined himself to the people of God, and became valiant for the truth as it is in Jesus. He soon after went to London, where he became intimate with Lord and Lady Dartmouth, Lady Gertrude Hotham, Lady Chesterfield, Romaine, and Whitefield. The latter says of him,

"He stands here in town against the opposition of his old companions like another Daniel; he must be, nay, he hath already been, thrown into a den of lions; but he hath One with him who can stop the lion's mouth." Berridge, Fletcher, and Venn were appointed his chaplains. "Though I feel not the least degree of value for any honour that cometh of man," said Venn to Lady Huntingdon, on receiving the appointment, "yet this pleases me very much, because I can receive it in no other light than that of bearing a public testimony that Jesus, the God of the Christians, is his God and his all."

Lady Anne Erskine, the eldest daughter of the house, a lady of exemplary piety, now made her home with Lady Huntingdon, a daughter in her affections, a partner in her toils, and a well-beloved sister in the Lord Jesus Christ.

The funeral services of the earl, with the faithful application made of them by the impressive oratory of Whitefield, produced a deep seriousness at Bath, and brought large numbers of the nobility to Lady Huntingdon's chapel. On the departure of Whitefield, she was anxious to follow up the impression already made with the powerful preaching of Venn and Berridge. She wrote in urgent terms to summon them to Bath.

"My lady," wrote Berridge from Everton, December 26, 1767, "I had a letter from your ladyship last Saturday, and another from Lord Buchan. His letter required an immediate answer, which I sent on Monday, and then went out a preaching. I am now returned, and sit down to answer yours. But what must I say? Verily you are a good piper, but I know not how to dance. I love your scorpion letters dearly, though they rake the flesh off my bones, and I believe your eyes are better than mine, but I cannot yet read with your glasses. I do know that I want quickening every day, but I do not see that I want a journey to Bath. I have been whipped pretty severely for fighting out of my own proper regiment, and for rambling out of the bounds of my rambles; and while the smart of the rod remains on my back it will weigh more with me than a thousand arguments. All marching officers are not general officers, and every one should search out the extent of his commission. A gospel minister who has a church will have a diocese annexed to it, and is only an overseer or bishop of that diocese; and let him, like faithful Grimshaw, look well to it. An evangelist who has no church, is a metropolitan or cosmopolitan, and may ramble all the kingdom, or all the world over; and these are more highly honoured than the other, though they are not always duly sensible of the honour. They are nearest to the apostolic character of any.

"But whom do you recommend to the care of my church? Is it not one Onesimus who ran away from Philemon? If the dean of Tottenham could not hold him in with a curb, how could the vicar of Everton guide him with a snaffle? I do not want a helper merely to stand up in my pulpit, but to ride round my district. And I fear my weekly circuits would not suit a London or a Bath divine, nor any tender evangelist that is environed in prunello. Long rides and miry roads in sharp weather; cold houses to sit in, with very moderate fuel, and three or four children roaring or rocking around you; coarse food; lumpy beds to lie in, and too short for the feet; stiff blankets, like boards, for covering; rise at five in the morning to preach; at seven, breakfast; at eight, mount a horse, with boots never cleaned, and then ride home praising God for all mercies. Sure I must stay till your academy is finished, before I get an assistant.

"But enough of these matters. Let us now talk of Jesus, whom I treat in my letters as I deal with him in my heart, crowd him into a corner, when the first place and the whole room belongeth of right to himself. He has been whispering, of late, that I cannot keep myself or the flock committed to me; but has not hinted a word as yet, that I do wrong in keeping close to my fold. And my instructions, you know, must come from the Lamb, not from the Lamb's wife, though she is a tight woman. He has taught me to labour for him more cheerfully, and to loathe myself more heartily, than I ever could before. I see myself nothing and feel myself vile, and hide my head, ashamed of all my sorry services. I want his fountain every day, his intercession every moment, and would not give a groat for the broadest fig-leaves or the brightest human rags to cover me. A robe I must have of one whole piece, broad as the law, spotless as the light, and richer than an angel ever wore – the robe of Jesus. And when the elder Brother's raiment is put on me, good Isaac will receive and bless the lying varlet Jacob."

12

Trevecca

AT THIS period there were many pious students both at Cambridge and Oxford; and although, as in the college days of Wesley and Whitefield, opprobrium and opposition were still to be encountered, yet there was now at length a larger circle of brave and good men throughout England to lend them sympathy and assistance. The Cambridge band was headed by Rowland Hill, who already began to exhibit that fearless zeal in the cause of truth, which afterwards rendered him so conspicuous.

In the bosom of Oxford, was also a little company in whose hearts glowed the fires of devotion, and who, not content with being saved themselves, went about in the by-ways and hamlets of the poor, striving if haply they might be instrumental in saving others. This excited the jealousy of the church, and the ridicule of their fellows. A storm was gathering, which, after a few threatening signs, burst upon the heads of six young men of St Edmund's Hall.

"A very odd affair has happened here," says a fellow of Baliol. "The principal of Edmund Hall has been indiscreet enough to admit into his hall, by the *recommendation of Lady Huntingdon,* seven London tradesmen; they have little or no learning, but have all of them a high opinion of themselves, as being ambassadors of 'King Jesus.' One of them, upon that title conferred by himself, has been a preacher. Complaint was made to the vice-chancellor, I believe, by the bishop of Oxford; and he, in his own right as vice-chancellor, had last week a visitation of the hall. Six of the preaching tradesmen were found so void of learning that they were expelled. He has done well in removing from hence some 'ambassadors of King Jesus,' who were likely to do more harm than good."

The expulsion is thus announced in the St James' Chronicle: "On Friday, March 11, 1768, six students belonging to Edmund Hall were expelled from the university, after a hearing of several hours before the vice-chancellor and some of the heads of the houses, for holding Methodistical tenets, and taking upon them to read, pray, and expound the Scriptures, and singing hymns in private houses. The principal of the college defended their doctrines from the thirty-nine articles of the established church, and spoke in the highest terms of the piety and exemplariness of their lives; but his motion was overruled, and sentence pronounced against them. One of the heads of houses present observed, that as these six gentlemen were expelled for having too much religion, – it would be very proper to inquire into the conduct of some who had too little; yet Mr Vice-Chancellor was heard to tell the chief accuser, that the university was much obliged to him for his good work."

"It is a grievous thing," exclaimed Lady Huntingdon, who looked on with a deep and painful interest, "to find men who have solemnly subscribed to the doctrines of the Reformation, acting with such inconsistent cruelty, tyranny, and falsehood towards those who conscientiously adhere to the tenets of our excellent church, and endeavour to propagate her principles."

This affair served to quicken Lady Huntingdon in maturing a project which she had long contemplated, of establishing a college for the purpose of training young men for the ministry; she had been led to the subject by finding how difficult it was to supply her chapels with needful help, and especially how impossible it was to enlarge her sphere of operations, under the existing embarrassments.

After much deliberation and the counsel of her wisest and choicest friends, the plan of a college was drawn up, into which only such young men should be admitted as students, as gave evidence of piety and were resolved to devote themselves to the work of the ministry; they were to remain three years at the institution, board and education gratuitous, to receive a new suit of clothes once a year, and on leaving might enter the established church or any other Protestant religious denomination. Here pious young men could be trained for the ministry unfettered by the peculiar restrictions of a university course, while very many might be qualified for usefulness who could ill afford a longer and more expensive pupillage.

Where should the new college be located? Trevecca was fixed upon, in the parish of Talgarth, South Wales. Perhaps not the least of the attractions of Trevecca might have been, that here dwelt Howell Harris, with no cooling of the holy fire, and no abatement of the Welsh vigour of his soul. But the frame which had braved summer heats and winter colds in his Master's service, had given way, and Harris sat waiting in his battered tent for the summons to go up higher.

Mr Venn, in one of his preaching tours, visited Trevecca, "happy Trevecca," as he calls it; and further adds, "Howell Harris is the father of that settlement, and the founder. After labouring for fifteen years more violently than any of the servants of Christ in this revival, he was so hurt in body as to be confined to his own house for seven years. Upon the beginning of this confinement, first one, and then another, whom the Lord had converted under his Word, to the number of near a hundred, came and desired to live with him, and they would work and get their bread. By this means, near one hundred and twenty men, women, and children, from very distant parts of Wales, came and fixed their tents at Trevecca. We were there three days, and heard their experience, which they spoke in Welsh to Mr Harris, and he interpreted to us. Of all the people I ever saw, this society seems to be the most advanced in grace. My heart received a blessing from them and their pastor, which will abide with me."

Trevecca, then, was to be the seat of the proposed college; and for this purpose, Lady Huntingdon took Trevecca House, a venerable structure dating back as far as 1176, and had it opened for religious and literary instruction, with a chapel dedicated to the worship of God, on the 24th of August, 1768. Mr Whitefield preached from the words, "In all places where I record my name, I will come unto thee, and bless thee." On the Sabbath following, he addressed a congregation of some thousands, assembled in the court before the house.

Mr Fletcher of Madely was appointed president, and shortly after, Rev John Benson head master of the institution.

While the project was approved and encouraged by most of Lady Huntingdon's friends, there were some who regarded it in a less favourable light, among whom was Mr Berridge. Lady Huntingdon resided at Trevecca the greater part of the year, and the "influence of her fervent piety," says one, "was highly beneficial. The spirit of devotion was everywhere apparent; when walking in the neighbouring vales, one might often hear from several parts of the surrounding woodlands the voice of social prayer, arising from little bands of students who were pouring out their hearts before God.

"Active exertion was united with devotional exercises; horses were kept for the purpose of conveying the students to more distant places on Saturday afternoons, while the nearer villages were visited on foot, and thus the benefits of the college were felt throughout the surrounding towns and villages, to the distance of twenty or thirty miles. Frequently a student was sent to greater distances to preach in certain *districts* or *rounds,* as they were termed. On these tours, chapels, private houses, market-places, or fields, as occasion required, became the scene of his labours; and by this missionary work was the gospel introduced, and the cause of Christ revived in very many places, where we now find flourishing churches."

For many years, the anniversaries of this college were scenes of deep and stirring interest. Vast crowds collected, sometimes numbering three thousand; and on one occasion no fewer than one thousand three hundred horses were turned into a large field adjoining the college, besides those that were stationed in the neighbouring villages. Baskets of bread and meat were distributed to the people in the court, while ample feasts of the bread of life were furnished by some of the most distinguished preachers of that day. The college was blessed by many tokens of the divine favour; extensive revivals of religion followed the labours both of teachers and pupils, until Mr Berridge, moved by the cheering news which ever and anon reached the Everton parsonage, was constrained to acknowledge the favourable change in his feelings, and so wrote to its patroness.

"*My Lady* – When the frost broke up I became miserable indeed, just able at times to peep into my Bible, but not able to endure the touch of a quill. I am now reviving, but not revived, and can venture to take up my pen; you will have its first-fruits, such as they are.

"I am glad to hear of the plentiful effusion from above on Talgarth. Jesus has now baptised your college, and thereby shown his approbation of the work; you may therefore rejoice, but rejoice with trembling. Faithful labourers may be expected from thence; but if it is Christ's college, a Judas will certainly be found among them. I believe the baptism will prove a lasting one, but I believe the sensible comfort will not always last as long. Neither is it convenient. In the present state of things, a winter is as much wanted to continue the earth fruitful as a summer. If the grass were always growing, it would soon grow to nothing; just as flowers that blow much and long, generally blow themselves to death. And as it is thus with the ground, so it is with the labourers too. Afflictions, desertions, and temptations are as needful as consolations. Jonah's whale will teach a good lesson, as well as Pisgah's top. I see Jonah come out of the whale cured of his rebellion; I see Moses go up to the mount with meekness, but come down in a huff and break the tables. Further, I see three picked disciples attending their Master to the mount, and fall asleep there.

"I believe you must be clad only in sackcloth while you tarry in the wilderness, and be a right mourning widow until the Bridegroom fetches you home. Jesus has given you a hand and a heart to execute great things for his glory, therefore he will deal you out a suitable measure of afflictions to keep your balance steady. Did Paul labour more abundantly than all his brethren? He had more abundant stripes than they all. The Master will always shave your crown before he puts a fresh coronet upon your head, and I expect to hear of a six months' illness when I hear of your building a new chapel.

"I cannot comfort you by saying that I think your day is almost spent, and that your afternoon shadows lengthen. Go on, my dear lady; build and fight manfully, and believe lustily. Look upward and press forward. Heaven's eternal hills are before you, and Jesus stands with arms wide open to receive you. One hour's sight and enjoyment of the Bridegroom in his place above, will make you forget all your troubles by the way. Yet a little while, and He that shall come, will come, and receive you with a heavenly welcome. Here we must purge and bleed, for physic is needful, and a tender Physician administers all. But the inhabitants of heaven cry out and sing, 'We are no more sick' –

> *"'Ah, Lord, with tardy steps I creep,*
> *And sometimes sing, and sometimes weep;*
> *Yet strip me of this trunk of clay,*
> *And I will sing as sweet as they.'*

"A very heavy time have I had for the last three weeks – cloudy days and moonless nights. Only a little consolation fetched down now and then by a little dull prayer. At times I am ready to wish that sin and the devil were both dead, they make such a horrible racket within me and about me. Rather let me pray, 'Lord, give me faith and patience; teach me to expect the cross daily, and help me to take it up cheerfully.' Woefully weary I am of myself, but know not how to live daily and feast upon Jesus. A treasure he is indeed, but lies hid in a field, and I know not how to dig in the dark. May daily showers from above fall on you and refresh you, and the dew of heaven light upon your chapels and college.

"I remain your affectionate servant in a loving Jesus,

"JOHN BERRIDGE"

Nor did Lady Huntingdon's friends rest in empty expressions of approbation, for these were often supported by bank-notes. We find recorded five hundred pounds, the second gift from John Thornton, towards defraying the expenses of the institution, and a thousand pounds from some female friends who loved the Lord. To Lady Glenorchy, who enclosed four hundred pounds, Lady Huntingdon writes,

"I am indeed bound to thank your ladyship most sincerely for your generous gift to the college, which has been the offspring of many tears and strong crying to the great and glorious Head of the church. This is surely one of the blessed effects of that faith wrought in your heart by the power of the Holy Ghost. The college is in a most glorious state. The unction of the Holy One is continually descending on its beloved inmates, and the love and harmony that reigns among them all, it is most delightful to witness. Fired with a zeal for God and perishing souls, all seem determined in their strength to spend and be spent in this divine employ. The college, as dear Mr Berridge says, has been baptised with the baptism of the Holy Ghost; great grace rests upon all within its walls, and eminent success crowns their labours in the towns and villages around. To God alone be all the glory. The work is his, and he will carry it on in his own way. His smiles of approbation have cheered my heart amidst the many cares, labours, and sorrows I have to contend with. I thirst for an entire devotedness to him, and his cause and interest in the world. O that I had a thousand hearts, a thousand hands; all should be employed for him, for he is worthy. Sing, O my soul, Worthy is the Lamb that was slain."

In the hearts of how many of God's professing people does this wish meet with an earnest and hearty response?

13

A New Recruit – Tunbridge Wells

" SIR – Mr Thomas Palmer was at my house last week, and desired me to call upon you when I went to Cambridge. I am now at Grandchester, a mile from you, where I preached last night and this morning, and where I shall abide until three in the afternoon; will you take a walk over? The weather is frosty, which makes it pleasant underfoot. If you love Jesus Christ, you will not be surprised at this freedom taken by a stranger, who seeks your acquaintance only out of love to Christ and his people.

"I am, for his sake, your affectionate servant,

"J. BERRIDGE"

This was addressed to the leader of the Cambridge band of pious youth, *Rowland Hill*, tidings of whose fearless fervour had reached the vicarage of Everton, only a few miles from Cambridge, and rejoiced the heart of its good old master. The invitation was thankfully responded to, and Rowland, a blooming young man of nineteen years, set out for Grandchester mill, where Berridge tarried with the miller. And thus these two met to confer together upon the rich prerogatives and ample endowments of their heavenly inheritance. Rowland's family were divided in their views of Christian duty. His elder brother Richard, and two of his sisters, sympathised with the religious movements of the day, and had themselves received a saving knowledge of the truth as it is in Jesus. For Rowland they had felt the deepest solicitude; for not only had he the common temptations which beset the path of a rich man's son, but he possessed a vivacity and wit which would not fail to fascinate and delight the lively circles of college students.

As the time of his quitting Hawkstone for school drew near, the language of their hearts was, "We *cannot* let thee go, without a blessing from on high:" nor were their fidelity and earnestness lost upon him; he saw and felt the exceeding sinfulness of sin, and laid hold of the Refuge provided in the gospel. The change which passed over him was a thorough and permanent one; there was no reserve in his consecration to Christ, and henceforth it became the endeavour and the delight of his life to make known to others that salvation which he had found so precious to his own soul. But upon this turn in the current of his life, his parents looked with a less favourable eye; they sought to arrest him in his new course. Nor were college tutors more lenient, nor college companions more merciful. Rowland endured the cross for his Master's sake. Among the students there were a few of like faith, and these stood firm, willing to endure reproach and contradiction with him for the sake of Christ.

From the meeting at the mill a delightful intimacy sprang up between the old disciple and the new, and every Sabbath, while at Cambridge, Rowland tried to spend a portion of the day at Everton.

Although a diligent student, and holding a high rank in his classes, the young man was more than a student: the musty air of a cloistered life did not suit the buoyant energies of his spirit; he craved the warmth and excitement of active life; he could not behold the moral wastes and the famishing poor in his daily walks, without longing to sow the seed and carry the bread of eternal life. And this he did. He pressed forward, doing with his might whatsoever his hand found to do. A strong opposition was raised against him. The faculty threatened, and his father frowned. In the midst of his troubles he ventured to address Mr Whitefield, then at London, and lay his perplexities before him.

"About thirty-four years ago," answered Whitefield, "the master of Pembroke College, where I was educated, took me to task for visiting the sick and going to the prisons. In my haste I said, 'Sir, if it displeaseth you, I go no more.' My heart smote me immediately. I repented, and went again: he heard of it – threatened, but for fear he should be looked upon as a persecutor, he let me alone. The hearts of all are in the Redeemer's hands. I would not have you give way, no, not for a moment; the storm is too great to hold long: visiting the sick and imprisoned, and instructing the ignorant, are the very vitals of true and undefiled religion. If threatened, or denied a degree, or expelled for *this,* it will be the best degree you can take: a glorious preparation for, and a blessed presage of future usefulness. I have seen the dreadful consequences of giving way and looking back. How many, for this wretched cowardice and fear of the cross, have been turned into pillars, not of useful but useless salt. Now is your time to prove the strength of Jesus yours. If opposition did not so much abound, your consolations would not so much abound. Blind as he is, Satan sees some great good coming on. We never prospered so much at Oxford, as when we were hissed at and reproached as we walked along the streets. That is a poor castle that a little stinking breath of Satan's vassals can throw down. Your house, I trust, is better founded. Is it not built upon a rock? Is not that rock the blessed Jesus? The gates of hell, therefore, shall not be able to prevail against it. Go on, therefore, my dear man, go on. Old Berridge, I believe, would give you the same advice. God be praised that you are helped to bless, while others blaspheme. God bless and direct and support you. Good Lady Huntingdon is in town. She will rejoice to hear that you are under the cross. You will not want her prayers, or the poor prayers of, my dear honest young friend,

"Yours in an all-conquering Jesus."

This letter, so much in harmony with his own feelings, encouraged and animated the young man to engage with fresh ardour in his labours of love.

Not long after this, in 1768, while under the displeasure of his father, he came to Bath, on his way to Cambridge, and paid a visit to Lady Huntingdon, who received the young evangelist with open arms. He preached at her chapel, and expounded in her house, with great acceptance, giving promise on every occasion of that salient oratory which distinguished his riper years.

Rowland Hill was now twenty-three, and ready to receive orders; yet six bishops refused to ordain him, on account of his irregular conduct at Cambridge, and for fear of still greater irregularities in time to come.

This, with divers other trials, grieved and embarrassed him: his father restricted his allowance, in hope of breaking up his preaching tours; but his spirit could neither be curbed nor broken. With his little Welsh pony, the gift of a friend, without purse or scrip, he went forth on the highways and by-ways, far and wide, proclaiming the unsearchable riches of Christ. "Make the best of your time," said Berridge; "while the Lord affords travelling health, and strong lungs, blow your horn soundly."

"I find you have got honest Rowland down to Bath," he writes to Lady Huntingdon once, while entertaining the ranger at her house. "He forsakes father and mother and brethren, and gives up all for Jesus. The Lord hath owned him much at Cambridge and in the north, and I hope will own him more abundantly in the west."

Lady Huntingdon's house at Bath became now for a time his headquarters, whence he went forth through the neighbouring towns, preaching to large crowds, receiving abuse, or welcome, as the world saw fit to give him.

"I think your chief work for a season will be," writes Berridge to him, "to break up fallow-ground. This suits the accent of your voice at present. God will give you other tongues, when they are wanted; but he now sends you out to thrash the mountains, and a glorious thrashing it is. Go forth, my dear Rowley, whenever you are invited, into the devil's territories; carry the Redeemer's standard along with you, and blow the gospel trumpet boldly, fearing nothing but your-self. If you meet with success, as I trust you will, expect clamours and threats from the world, and a little sorrow now and then from the children. These bitter herbs make good sauce for a young recruiting sergeant, whose heart would be lifted up with pride, if it were not kept down by these pressures. Make the Scriptures your only study, and be much in prayer. The apostles gave themselves to the Word of God, and to prayer. Do thou likewise. Labour to keep your mind in a heavenly frame; it will make your work pleasant, and your conver-sation savoury. Now is your time to work for Jesus. You have health and youth on your side, and no church or wife on your back. The world is all before you, and Providence your guide and guard. Fear not. Jesus is with you."

The encouragement and countenance thus cordially proffered to the young Rowland by these veterans in his Master's service, Berridge and Whitefield, falling happily in with the current of his own tastes and talents, confirmed the sturdy catholicism of his views: and as they were about departing from the field, they cast on the young recruit the mantle of their own resolute, yet tolerant and loving spirit, which had made their preaching awful as that of the Hebrew prophet, and winning as that of the beloved disciple.

Let us now pass to Tunbridge Wells, in the county of Kent, thirty-five miles south-east of London, a town much resorted to by the sick for the healing power of its waters, and by the fashionable to banish time and ennui by the picturesque beauties and the unrestrained gaieties which the place afforded.

The cloud of mercies which broke upon Brighton and Oathall, led Lady Huntingdon to hope also something for so unpromising a field as Tunbridge Wells; and she was encouraged in this by Sir Thomas L'Anson, a pious man, who lived in the neighbourhood, and who had sometimes opened his own mansion to the preaching of the gospel. She went hither, accompanied by Mr Venn and Mr Madan, in 1763, when large meetings were held in the Presbyterian church. But spacious as was the place, thousands were unable to get in. To satisfy the eager interest of the people, Lady Huntingdon begged them to take the open field, a new and extraordinary spectacle to the people of Tunbridge Wells, and it created no small stir both among townsfolk and visitors.

"May the precious name of Him who died to save, be made very dear to many in this place, and may this grain of mustard-seed become, by the blessing of God, a flourishing tree, extending its branches far and wide," was the parting benediction of one of the preachers. And that the grain began to spring up, and other of the Lord's husbandmen came and cared for the shoots, we may fairly conclude, for, five years afterwards, we find Lady Huntingdon taking up a permanent residence on Mount Ephraim, one of the three little hills between which the town is situated, with Whitefield by her side. This was in the summer of 1768.

During the following winter, Lady Huntingdon spent a few months in London at her house in Portland Row, Cavendish Square. Anxiety and her incessant labours threw her upon a sick-bed, and confined her for many weeks to the house; but though it suspended her personal activity, it did not close her doors to the preaching of the gospel. Whitefield, Wesley, and Romaine are there, "holding forth the word of life" to as large auditories of the nobility and fashion of the metropolis, as in the earlier days of their ministrations. Whitefield was labouring under severe bodily suffering, yet his labours were abundant, and in every interval of ease he was as alert as a watchman on a beleaguered city. In March, Mr Venn arrived at London, where he found a warm welcome and hospitable entertainment at Portland Row. He was anxious to improve every opportunity of attending upon this great evangelist, whose conversation and ministry were so filled with an unction from on high, and whose failing health gave mournful presage that the places now so glad with his presence must soon know him no more for ever. At the last meeting at Lady Huntingdon's house for the season, we find Charles Wesley the preacher, Romaine and Venn are administering the Lord's Supper, and Whitefield pouring out his soul in the parting prayer with unspeakable solemnity, as though his feet had already touched the waters of Jordan.

Lady Huntingdon immediately proceeded to Bath in company with Mr Venn. Lady Fanny Shirley, Lady Gertrude Hotham, and the Countess of Buchan now resided here, shedding a religious influence over the circles in which they moved, and striving to commend the Christian profession not only by well-ordered lives, but by seeking to bring their friends to a like precious experience.

The chapel, which had been fully attended during the winter, was now supplied for a few Sabbaths by Mr Venn. In his correspondence at this time, among other interesting things, he writes thus: "I am favoured with the pleasing sight, and with the animating example of a soul inflamed with love to a crucified God, that stumbling-block to them that perish. In Lady Huntingdon I see a star of the first magnitude in the firmament of the church. Blessed be God for free grace, that salvation is to every one that cometh to Christ. Otherwise, when I compare my life and my spirit with hers, I could not believe the same heaven was to contain us. How do works, the works of faith and love, speak and preach Jesus Christ, in that devoted servant of his. No equipage, no livery servants, no house, all these given up, that perishing sinners may hear the life-giving sound, and be enriched with all spiritual blessings. Her prayers are heard, her chapel is crowded, and many sinners among the poor are brought to the city of refuge. I feel, from Lady Huntingdon's example, an increasing desire both for myself and you, and all our friends, that we may be active and eminent in the life of grace. Too apt are we to rest in life received, and not to be doing every day something for our Lord; either earnestly engaged in prayer, speaking affectionately to sinners, overcoming our selfish passions, or exercising mercy to our needy brethren; but it is by *abounding in every good work,* that our light shines before men, and we stand confessed the workmanship of God in Christ.

"I have enjoyed in this visit the edifying discourse and bright example of many of our dear Saviour's family, all of them partakers of one life and one spirit, yet each distinguished by its particular hue and beauteous colour more predominant than the rest. In one, I have been animated by the ardent activity for the glory of Christ and the salvation of souls. In another, I was pleased and softened by conspicuous meekness and gentleness of spirit. In a third, I was excited to love and good works, by the fervent charity and brotherly kindness I beheld; and in a fourth, I was led to abase myself, and confess the pride of my heart, from the humility and brokenness of spirit that struck me. In the Head alone, all graces in their lustre unite."

How lovely is Christian fellowship, thus reflecting and multiplying the Christian graces.

In April, Whitefield left London, and followed Lady Huntingdon to Bath; his health becoming somewhat improved, accompanied by the Countess and Lady Anne Erskine, he made a tour through Bristol, Chippenham, Rodborough, Gloucester, Cheltenham, and several other towns, the scenes of early and later triumphs. "Never were these places so endeared to me," he exclaimed. "Old friends, old gospel wine, and the great Governor ordering to fill to the brim! Oh, to grace what mighty debtors!"

In May, the three, with the addition of Lady Buchan and Miss Orton, proceeded to Tunbridge Wells, to attend the dedication of the chapel, now nearly completed. At an early hour on the Sabbath morning of the services, great numbers assembled in the court before the countess' residence, to begin the day with prayer and praise.

"It is impossible," exclaimed the lady of the mansion, "to express the delight and satisfaction I felt, on being awoke at an early hour in the morning by the voice of praise and thanksgiving; my heart was powerfully affected, and never shall I forget the pleasure I then experienced."

These tokens of interest and religious fervour must have been peculiarly welcome, for they were blossoming from the little seed long since sown, and foreshadowings of a precious and golden harvest yet to be reaped. At the opening services, the prayers of the established church were read by Mr De Courcy, and Mr Whitefield preached the sermon; but the chapel having become crowded almost to suffocation, the sermon was delivered in the open air, from a mound in the court before the chapel. It was one of his most eloquent and thrilling efforts; the lofty energy of his tones, the utter forgetfulness of himself in the all-absorbing interest of his subject, the very impersonation of the truths which he uttered as he stretched forth his hand – "Look yonder; what is that I see? It is my agonising Lord! Hark, hark; do not you hear? O earth, earth, earth, hear the Word of the Lord!" thrilled the vast congregation, riveting the eye, piercing the conscience, and holding strong men breathless before the resistless might of his oratory.

Infirm, asthmatic, corpulent, and heavy, Whitefield has lost none of his early power; the grace and elasticity of both youth and health have gone, field preaching has lost the freshness and strangeness of thirty years before; his themes have no new elements, his mind no broader range, his thoughts no sharper cut or richer mould, yet he is Whitefield still, with all his out-gushing eloquence, thronged by a crowd, who hung with eager and trembling earnestness upon his august and impassioned utterances. The unabated popularity of this wonderful man is one of the most remarkable things in his history; when we remember, too, that he founded no sect, led off no followers, opened no new school of Theology, and protested against no system. He was upheld or carried forward by no partisan interest of any kind. It was eminently a *personal power* which he wielded, receiving neither force nor abatement from patronage or party. What this power precisely was, it is perhaps difficult to decide. Vividness of conception, singleness of aim, depth of emotion, a native tenderness of spirit, all concentrated upon one grand theme, and that theme *Christ, the crucified and risen Saviour;* and more than all this, his being a chosen instrument in this spiritual renewal of the true church, set apart by the Lord of glory – herein were the hidings of his power.

14

The Breach

THE first day of the year 1770 Lady Huntingdon set apart for fasting and prayer, and for a renewed dedication of herself to God. "I am just returned from the Lock," she says in the evening, "where I heard a profitable sermon from dear Mr Romaine on that awful passage, 'This year thou shalt die.' If the Lord shall see fit to remove me hence the year just begun, may my worthless soul be numbered with the redeemed before his throne. Of late I have enjoyed much intimate fellowship with the Father and the Son, and the Holy Ghost has frequently witnessed with my spirit that I am his child. This has caused me to rejoice with unspeakable joy."

Such are the delights which are the privilege of the Christian. How do they cheer and soothe the soul chafed by the disappointments and cares that must needs beset us in our earthly pilgrimage. In proportion as our sphere is wide, so do cares multiply, and we live to see the fairest mornings clouded and our dearest hopes withered in the bud; drought blights our labours, and barrenness eats up our Edens. It was in such a season of suspended fruitfulness that this pious woman had written to Berridge; and to her letter, under the date of January 9, he thus replies:

"You complain that every new work after a season becomes a lifeless work. And was it not in the beginning as it is now? Do not the Acts and epistles show that the primitive churches much resembled our own? In their infancy we find them of one heart and soul, having all things common; but presently read of partial distribution in their church stock, then of eager and lasting contentions about circumcision, coupling Moses with Jesus, and setting a servant on a level with his Master. And Gentile churches are much on a level with the Jewish. The Corinthians soon fell into parties about their leaders, into errors about the resurrection, and into many gross immoralities. The Galatians seemed at first ready to present Paul with their own eyes, but grew desirous at last of plucking out his. The Ephesians had been much tossed by winds of doctrine. The Colossians had fallen into will-worship, and the Thessalonians had some of our gossips among them who would not work, but sauntered about picking up news and telling tales. Paul's labours were much employed in Asia, and many churches were gathered there; yet I hear him complaining in a certain place, that 'all they in Asia were turned aside from him.' Scripture mentions a former and a latter rain, between which of course there must have been an interval of drought and barrenness. The former rain falls just after seed-time, when there is plenty of manna coming down from above, plenty of honey flowing out of the rock, and plenty of joyful hosannas rising up to Jesus. After this rain comes the *interval,* during which most of the stony and thorny grounds sheer off, taking a final leave of Jesus; and the good grounds are scarcely discernible, so cold they appear and full of weeds, so exceedingly cold and swampy. At length the Lord ariseth in just indignation to chastise and vex his people, continuing his plagues until he has broken their bones and humbled their hearts, causing them to see and feel and loathe their backslidings, and raising up a sigh and a cry in their hearts for deliverance. Then comes the latter rain to revive and settle; after which they learn to walk humbly with God."

What church has not experienced this spiritual drought, when the leaves fall from the fig-tree and the vine fainteth for want of water? If the laws of the natural world are types and shadows of the spiritual, then such things must needs be in the present economy of life. And though we see but through a glass darkly, we discern a heavenly wisdom: those which have no root wither away, while the strong trunk abides the heat, and the delicate flower folds its leaves and bows its head, waiting meekly for the rain; these shall be for the garden of the Lord. Blessed are those who endure to the end.

It was in August of this year that the churches in connection with Mr Wesley held their twenty-seventh annual conference in London, which gave birth to a controversy, perhaps one of the hottest and most barren of spoils in the annals of Protestant theology. It was a kindling of the old flames that so nearly consumed the friendship of Wesley and Whitefield more than twenty years before; and though smothered for a season by the predominance of the Christian element, theological differences which marked their preaching were likely to assume a greater importance in the minds of their friends or followers, and demand a more unqualified acknowledgment. The conference made the following declarations:

"1. With regard to *men's faithfulness.* Our Lord himself taught us to use the expression, therefore we ought never to be ashamed of it. We ought steadily to assert, upon his authority, that if a man is not *faithful in the unrighteous mammon,* God *will not give him the true riches.*

"2. With regard to *working for life,* which our Lord expressly commands us to do. Labour, *work for the meat that endureth to everlasting life.* And in fact every believer, till he comes to glory, works *for* as well as *from* life.

"3. We have received it as a maxim, that 'a man is to do nothing in order to justification.' Nothing can be more false. Whoever desires to find favour with God, should *cease from evil and learn to do well.* So God himself teaches by the prophet Isaiah. Whosoever repents, *should do works meet for repentance.* And if this is not in order to find favour, what does he do it for?

"In review,

"1. Who of us is *now* accepted of God?

"He that now believes in Christ with a loving and obedient heart.

"2. But who among those that never heard of Christ?

"He that, according to the light he has, feareth God and worketh righteousness.

"3. Is this the same with him that is sincere?

"Nearly, if not quite.

"4. Is not this salvation by works?

"Not by the *merit* of works, but by works as a condition.

"5. What then have we been disputing about these thirty years?

"I am afraid, about words.

"6. As to the *merit,* of which we have been so dreadfully afraid, we are rewarded *according to our works,* yea, *because of our works.* How does this differ from, *for the sake of our works?* Can you split this hair?

"7. The grand objection to one of the preceding doctrines is drawn from matter of fact. God does in fact justify those who, by their own confession, neither *feared God* nor *wrought righteousness*. Is this an exception to the general rule? It is a doubt whether God makes any exception at all. But how are we sure that the person in question never did fear God or work righteousness? His own saying so is no proof; for we know how all that are convinced of sin undervalue themselves in this respect.

"8. Does not talking of a *justified* or a *sanctified state* tend to mislead men? almost naturally leading them to trust in what was done at one moment? Whereas we are, every hour and every moment, pleasing or displeasing to God 'according to our works,' according to the whole of our inward tempers and our outward behaviour."

These were the minutes which alarmed Lady Huntingdon and her friends, because they were thought to be aimed against divine sovereignty and electing grace, which were favourite doctrines of Mr Whitefield and his adherents. With an honest though hasty warmth, Lady Huntingdon declared that no one embracing the statements laid down in these minutes could remain in her college. Mr Benson, her head-teacher, defended them, and in consequence closed his connection with the college.

"I am glad you had courage," said Wesley to him, "to speak your mind on so critical an occasion. At all hazards do so still, only with all possible tenderness and respect. She is much devoted to God, and has a thousand valuable and amiable qualities."

Mr Benson immediately informed Mr Fletcher, the President, of his dismissal, who says, with his wonted tenderness for those who love the Lord, "Take care, my dear sir, not to make matters worse than they are; cast the mantle of forgiving love over circumstances that might injure the cause of God, so far as it is put into the hands of that eminent lady, who hath so well deserved of the church of Christ; but if what you say is true, a false step has been taken, and if the plan of the college is overthrown, I have nothing more to say to it."

A circular was now issued by the offended party inviting the clergy of all denominations to convene at Bristol, in order to meet the Wesleyan conference, and compel them to retract their heresies. The tone of the circular was more calculated to aggravate than to conciliate. The evening before the meeting took place, Lady Huntingdon wrote to Wesley apologising for any seeming harshness or imperiousness: "As Christians," she says, "we wish to retract what a more deliberate consideration might have prevented, as we would as little wish to defend even truth itself presumptuously, as we would submit servilely to deny it."

The two parties met; a candid and Christian temper presided over the discussions, and mutual explanations and concessions took place; Lady Huntingdon's chaplains and friends acknowledging an indiscreet haste in making up and expressing their opinions, and Wesley consenting to make such a public explanation of his views as would satisfy the unbiased mind.

"Whereas," he says, "the doctrinal points in the minutes of a conference held in London, August 7, 1770, have been understood to favour justification by works; now we, the Rev John Wesley and others, assembled in conference, do declare we had no such meaning, and that we abhor the doctrine of justification by works as a most perilous and abominable doctrine. And as the said minutes are not sufficiently guarded in the way they are expressed, we hereby solemnly declare in the sight of God, that we have no trust or confidence but in the alone merits of our Lord and Saviour Jesus Christ, for justification or salvation, either in life, death, or the Day of Judgment; and though no one is a real believer who doeth not good works when there is time and opportunity, yet our works have no part in meriting or purchasing our justification, from first to last, either in whole or in part." And thus it stands, signed by fifty-three of his preachers.

This frank and manly avowal, or disavowal, quieted the apprehensions of his friends; and peace must have been speedily restored between the two religious parties, had not a vindication of the doctrines of the minutes, prepared by Mr Fletcher at the request of Mr Wesley, and written before the meeting of the conference of adjustment, soon appeared. When Fletcher heard the result of the meeting at Bristol, he was extremely anxious to suppress the article; but it fell into the hands of a violent partisan, who hastened it through the press, and the gauntlet being thus thrown down, combatants were not wanting to take the field.

The details of this warfare it is hardly necessary to record here. Sir Richard Hill, Rev Augustus Toplady, and Mr Berridge were the principal writers on one side; Fletcher, Sellon, and Olivers on the other. However powerful may have been the arguments wielded on either side, tools also of a sharper point were freely used; acrimonious and intemperate expressions were hurled back and forth; both parties, instead of convincing or retreating, were driven to the extremes of their own principles, and made unguarded assertions of themselves and their opponents, the effect of which was to alienate the hearts of Christian brethren, draw them from their proper work, and widen the breach between those who really loved the Lord. Mr Thornton and others tried to pacify the parties, and moderate some of their excesses, but it availed little. Wesley took no active part in the war; and Fletcher, though one of the principal actors, must be allowed to have preserved the habitual serenity of his spirit; he was indeed, in a measure, above the storms of earthly passions. While in the heat of the controversy he came to Stoke Newington seriously indisposed, where he was visited by many distinguished people and several of his opponents. "I went to see a man with one foot in the grave," said one of him, "but I found a man with one foot in heaven."

"Your ladyship's account of what occurred at Mr Wesley's last conference does not surprise me," wrote Lady Glenorchy from Edinburgh; "May the Lord God of Israel be with you, and enable you to make a firm stand in defence of a free-grace gospel. Lady Anne's letter told me all you had been doing in this momentous affair. When you next write to dear Mr Shirley, give my kindest regards to him, and also to Mr Fletcher, Mr Venn, and Mr Romaine. May we all be kept by the mighty power of God unto the day of salvation.

"I am rejoiced at the success which has attended the college and your very extensive field of labour. I long to be more actively engaged for God, but hitherto my way has been greatly hedged up. When the weather permits, I frequently visit the poor, and find much liberty and pleasure in speaking for God. Knowing the great demands upon your generosity, I beg your acceptance of the enclosed for four hundred pounds, which you will oblige me by expending in that glorious cause which my heart longs to serve; and at the same time allow me to repeat, what I have already assured your ladyship, that my purse is always at your command, as I feel persuaded that the Lord smiles on your plans of usefulness and will crown them with his blessing."

A writer, describing these polemics, speaks of Berridge as a "buffoon as well as a fanatic," neither a very impartial nor discerning estimate of one of the noblest spirits of his day. We might, indeed, sometimes regret the indulgence of his humour, and could wish, for his vocation's sake, a check-rein to the bridle of his speech; but we fear we should have continued to laugh with him, instead of giving him the highest and noblest proof of our love for him and for Christ's cause, shown by Mr John Thornton in the following letter – a letter worthy of serious perusal by every clergyman whose wit is liable to get the better of his wisdom.

"In some discussions we have had relative to '*The Christian World Unmasked*,'" discourses Mr Thornton, "I could not help laughing with you, though at the same time I felt a check within; your reasons silenced, but did not satisfy me. Your vein of humour and mine seem much alike. If there is any difference between us, it lies here: I would strive against mine, while you seem to indulge yours. I fight against mine, because I find the ludicrous spirit is just as dangerous as the sullen one; and it is much the same to our great adversary, whether he falls in with a capricious, or facetious turn of mind. I could not forbear smiling at your humorous allegory about the tooth, and was pleased at the good sense displayed in it; yet something came across my mind – is this method agreeable to the idea we ought to entertain of a father in Israel? It would pass mighty well in a newspaper, or anything calculated for public entertainment; but it certainly wanted that solidity or seriousness that a Christian minister should write with. What the apostle said in another sense will apply here: 'When I was a child, I spake as a child,' etc. An expression of yours in your prayer before the sermon, when at Tottenham Court, struck me, that *God would give us* NEW *bread, not stale, but what was baked in the oven that day.* Whether it is that I am too little, or you too much used to such expressions, I won't pretend to determine, but I could not help thinking it savoured of attention to men more than to God. I know the apology frequently made for such language is, that the common people require it; it fixes their attention, and it affords matter for conversation afterwards; for a sentence out of the common road is more remembered than all the rest.

"This may be true, but the effect it has is only a loud laugh among their acquaintances; not one person is edified, and many are offended by such like expressions. Some ministers I have known, run into the other extreme, and think something grand must be uttered to strike the audience; but this seems to me as unnecessary as the other, and both have a twang of self-conceit, and seem like leaning to carnal wisdom. Truth, simple truth, requires no embellishments, nor should it be degraded; we are not to add or to take from it, but to remember the power is of God wholly.

"My reverend friend, as an old man, might be indulged in his favourite peculiarities if they would stop with him; but others catch the infection, and we find young ministers and common people indulging themselves in the same way; they think they are authorised so to do by such an example. Wit in any person is dangerous and often mischievous when used improperly, and especially on religious subjects; for as the professing part of an audience will much longer retain a witty or low expression than one more serious, so will the wicked part of it too, and turn it to the disadvantage of religion. I recollect but one humorous passage in all the Bible, which is that of Elijah with the Baalites; and when the time, place, and circumstances are properly considered, nothing could be more seasonable, nothing so effectually expose the impotency of their false god, and the absurdity of their vain worship. The prophets often speak ironically, sometimes satirically, but I do not remember of their ever speaking ludicrously. Our Lord and his apostles never had recourse to any such methods. The short abstracts we have of their sermons and conversations are all in a serious strain, and ministers cannot copy after a better example. I dare not say that giving liberty to a man's natural turn, or an endeavour to put and keep the people in good-humour, is sinful; but this I may assert, such a method is universally followed on the stage, and in all places of public entertainment, and therefore it seems to me to savour much more of the old man than of the new.

"I remember you once jocularly informed me you were born with a fool's cap on; pray, my dear sir, is it not high time it was pulled off? Such an accoutrement may suit a natural birth, and be of service; but surely it has nothing to do with a spiritual one, nor ever can be made ornamental to a serious man, much less to a Christian minister. I waive mentioning scripture injunctions, such as, 'Let your speech be with grace,' and so on, as you know these better than I do. Surely they should have some weight, for idle and unprofitable words stand forbidden. If it should please God to give you to see things as I do, you will think it necessary to be more guarded; but should you think me mistaken, I trust it will make no interruption with our friendship that I am thus free with you, as it proceeds from a sincere love and regard. The Tabernacle people are in general wild and enthusiastic, and delight in anything out of the common course, which is a temper of mind, though in some respects necessary, yet that should never be encouraged. If you and some few others, who have the greatest influence over them, would use the curb instead of the spur, I am persuaded the effect would be very blessed. Wildfire is better than no fire; but there is a divine warmth between these two extremes which the real Christian catches, and which when obtained is evidenced by a cool head and a warm heart, and makes him a glorious, shining example to all around him. I desire to be earnest in prayer that we may be more and more partakers of this heavenly wisdom, and ascribe all might, majesty, and dominion, to the Lord alone.

"I am, dear sir, yours affectionately,

"JOHN THORNTON"

"Dear and honoured sir," replies the vicar, "your favour of the 17th requires an answer attended with a challenge; and I do hereby challenge you, and defy all your acquaintances to prove, that I have a single correspondent half so honest as yourself. Epistolary intercourses are become a polite traffic, and he that can say pretty things, and wink at bad things, is an admired correspondent. Indeed, for want of due authority and meekness on one side, and of patience and humility on the other, to give or to take reproof, a fear of raising indignation instead of conviction, often puts a bar on the door of my lips; for I find where reproof does not humble it hardens, and the seasonable time of striking, if we can catch it, is when the iron is hot: when the heart is melted down in a furnace, then it submits to the stroke, and takes and retains the impression. I wish you would exercise the trade of a gospel limner, and draw the features of all my brethren in black, and send them their portraits. I believe you would do them justice every way, by giving every cheek its proper blush without hiding a dimple upon it. Yet I fear, if your subsistence depended on this business, you would often want a morsel of bread, unless I sent you a quartern loaf from Everton.

"As to myself, you know the man: odd things break from me as abruptly as croaking from a raven. I was born with a fool's cap. True, you say; yet why is not the cap put off? It suits the first Adam, but not the second. A very proper question, and my answer is this: a fool's cap is not put off so readily as a nightcap. One cleaves to the head, and one to the heart. Not many prayers only, but many furnaces, are needful for this purpose. And after all, the same thing happens to a tainted heart as to a tainted cask, which may be sweetened by many washings and firings, yet a scent remains still. Late furnaces have singed the bonnet of my cap, but the crown still abides on my head; and I must confess that the crown so abides, in whole or in part, for want of a closer walk with God, and nearer communion with him. When I creep near the throne, this humour disappears, or is tempered so well as not to be distasteful. Hear, sir, how my Master deals with me: when I am running wild, and saying things somewhat rash or very quaint, he gives me an immediate blow on my breast, which stuns me. Such a check I received while I was uttering that expression in prayer you complained of; but the bolt was too far shot to be recovered. Thus I had intelligence from above, before I received it from your hand. However, I am bound to thank you, and do hereby acknowledge myself reimbursed for returning your note.

"And now, dear sir, having given you an honest account of myself, and acknowledged the obligation I owe you, I would return the obligation in the best manner I am able. It has been a matter of surprise to me how Dr Conyers could accept of Deptford living, and how Mr Thornton could present him to it. The Lord says, 'Woe to the idle shepherd that leaveth his flock.' Is not Helmsley a flock, and a choice flock too, left – left altogether, and left in the hands, not of shepherds to feed, but of wolves to devour them? Has not lucre led him to Deptford, and has not a family connection overruled your private judgment? You may give me a box on the ear for these questions, if you please, and I will take it kindly, and still love and pray for you.

"The Lord bless you, and bless your family, and bless your affectionate servant,

"JOHN BERRIDGE"

15
Death of Whitefield

WHITEFIELD, though sick and infirm, was impelled by the strong current of his Christian sympathies to revisit America. He had been now four years in England, and his heart yearned with unspeakable tenderness for his dear children over the waters. "Besides," he says, "a pilgrim life is to me the sweetest this side of eternity; I am more content with it, and I shall have time enough to rest in heaven."

As the time of his departure drew near, more than ordinary tenderness and solemnity mingled with his leave-takings. "Oh these partings," he exclaimed; "without a divine support, they would be intolerable, Paul could stand a whipping-post, but not a weeping farewell."

On the day of his leaving London, he preached at the Tabernacle at seven in the morning; none too early for the friends and admirers of this distinguished man to grope their way through the damp and dingy atmosphere of an early London morning, responsive to his call.

"Oh, sinners, you are come to hear a poor creature take his last farewell; but I want you to forget the creature and his preaching. I want to lead you *further* than the Tabernacle, even to mount Calvary, to see with what expense of blood Jesus Christ purchased his own. Now, before I go any further, will you be so good, before the *world* gets into your hearts, to inquire whether you belong to Christ or not? Surely the *world* did not get into your hearts before you rose from your beds. Many of you were up sooner than usual. I hope the world does not get into your hearts before *nine*. Man, woman, sinner, put thy hand upon thy heart and say, didst thou ever hear Christ's voice so as to follow him?"

Thus, with apostolic fervency and colloquial directness, did he plead for the last time on behalf of the immortal interests of his Tabernacle auditory. There were heavy hearts and tearful eyes, even among strong men; while a cloud of heavenly benediction went up from grateful souls which had been made glad by his messages of love.

A large number of his friends, in coaches and on horseback, accompanied him to Gravesend, where he embarked on the last of September, 1769. Contrary winds detained the vessel some days along the coast, affording several opportunities for Whitefield to land and preach yet again on the dear old English soil. Favouring breezes at last sprang up, and his native land faded for ever from his sight. After a long and tedious passage, his thirteenth across the Atlantic, the Friendship arrived off Charleston the first of December, and a cordial welcome awaited him on shore. "Grace, grace!" ejaculates Whitefield; "a reception as hearty or heartier than ever. Blessed be God, I am brave and well, and am able to preach this afternoon."

As soon as possible he hastened to visit his Orphan-house at Bethesda. "Oh Bethesda, my Bethel, my Peniel!" he exclaims; "My happiness is inconceivable. I have had nine or ten prizes lately – you know what I mean – nine or ten orphans have been lately taken in. Hallelujah!"

For thirty years the Orphan-house had been the child of his love, the object of his paternal care, and the one thing which he felt anxious to provide for. An infirmary had been added to it, to which the poor and disabled resorted for charitable assistance, and at one time the number of patients amounted to one hundred and thirty. Although we find there was much land attached to the institution, a garden filled with "all sorts of greens," "plenty of milk, eggs, and poultry," sheep and cattle and horses, yet it was far from self-supporting; it seems always to have been attended with a heavy expense to the founder, who every year was compelled to tax the Christian public for its support.

Bethesda, however, wore an unusually flourishing aspect when now visited by Whitefield, and he immediately set about projecting a plan to increase its range of usefulness by adding a college; and "thus, may it please your excellency," runs his memorial to the governor of Georgia, "my beloved Bethesda will not only be continued a house of mercy to poor orphans, but be confirmed as a seat and nursery of sound learning and religious education, I trust, to the latest posterity." We find the following notice in the Georgia Gazette, bearing date, Savannah, January 31, 1770:

"Last Sunday, his excellency the governor, council, and assembly, having been invited by the Rev George Whitefield, attended divine service in the chapel of the Orphan-house academy, where prayers were read by the Rev Mr Ellington, and a very suitable sermon was preached by the Rev Mr Whitefield, from *Zechariah 4:9, 10:* 'The hands of Zerubbabel have laid the foundation of this house; his hands shall also finish it; and thou shalt know that the Lord of hosts hath sent me unto you; for who hath despised the day of small things?' to the general satisfaction of his auditory. After divine service, the company were very politely entertained with a plentiful and handsome dinner, and were greatly pleased to see the useful improvements made in the house in so much forwardness, and the whole executed with taste and in a masterly manner; and being sensible of the truly generous and disinterested benefactions derived to the province through his means, they expressed their gratitude in the most respectful terms."

In whatever light the plan of a college was regarded by the colonial authorities, no measures were ever taken towards putting it into execution during the lifetime of Whitefield; and after his death, one disaster after another swept away everything but the memory and the name of the Orphan-house of Georgia.

As soon as the news of Whitefield's return to the colonies had spread abroad, pressing invitations from the north poured in upon him, while the cordiality of his Georgia friends, and the apparent prosperity of his Bethesda, tempted him to remain at the south; "but no resting this side of eternity," he exclaimed; "all must give way to that divine employ, gospel ranging." Accordingly, when spring opens, we follow him to Philadelphia, "where pulpits, hearts, and affections seemed to be as open and enlarged towards him as ever;" and "notwithstanding I preach twice on the Lord's Day, and three or four times a week," he tells us, "I am better than I have been for many years."

He worked hard all summer, feeble as he was, with a fixed and unfaltering purpose to spend and be spent in the service of his Lord. From Philadelphia we track him to New York, wind with him up the Hudson and the Mohawk, project with him a missionary tour among the benighted Oneidas, tarry with him at Northampton, welcome him to Boston, and with anxious glance behold him, "faint yet rejoicing," start on a journey from that city to the east.

Everywhere his heart and hands are full; people flock to hear him; he has lost nothing of the forceful oratory of thirty years before: the heart is moved, the conscience pierced, and in spite of the abuse and misrepresentation which frequently beset his path, his presence is reverently sought for, his coming eagerly expected, his arrival cordially welcomed, and his "journeyings oft" are like a march of triumph through the land. Sorely worn and weary is the outward, yet is the inward life struggling for utterance and action. Now he is compelled to pause and recruit his decaying powers; the next day he starts up from the suffering couch as with a fresh lease of health.

"You will see," he writes from Portsmouth, New Hampshire, and it was his last letter, "by the many invitations, what a door is opened for preaching the everlasting gospel. I was so ill on Friday that I could not preach, though thousands were waiting to hear. Well, the day of release will shortly come; but it does not seem yet, for by riding sixty miles I am better, and hope to preach here tomorrow. I trust my blessed Master will accept of these poor efforts to serve him. Oh, for a warm heart. Oh, to stand fast in the faith; to quit ourselves like men, and be strong."

On a beautiful Saturday in the latter part of September, he rode from Portsmouth to Exeter, where he was expected, and preached to a great multitude already assembled in the fields beneath a rich autumnal sky, and surrounded by the golden harvest. Before going out, someone remarked he was more fit to go to bed than to preach.

"True, sir," replied the almost dying man, who turned aside, and clasping his hands, ejaculated, "Lord Jesus, I am weary *in* thy work, but not *of* it. If I have not yet finished my course, let me go and speak for thee once more in the field, seal thy truth, and come home to die;" and it seemed like prophetic prayer: once more he went forth, and the forests rang with the melody of his tones, and men hung on his words as if they had been the words of an angel.

After dining with Captain Gilman, he rode to Newburyport. The evening shadows of his brilliant day were fast lengthening around him. Night overtook him in the cold damps of death, and the

Sabbath dawn witnessed his departure to an eternal Sabbath in the heavens. His death was sudden and unexpected. Though known to be sick, his ceaseless activity made men forget his infirmities, and the pause in his career was abrupt and startling. This event occurred September 30, 1770.

Everywhere good men made great lamentation over him.

Mr Sherburne of Portsmouth immediately sent to Rev Mr Parsons, at whose house he died, to beg the body for his own new tomb; several gentlemen also came from Boston to ask for the remains of one so dear to the churches; but mindful of Whitefield's often expressed desire, should he die at Newburyport, that he might be buried before the pulpit of his friend, Mr Parsons declined these requests, and the great evangelist lies interred in the Federal Street church, where a handsome cenotaph has been erected to his memory.

The funeral services were most solemn and affecting, for multitudes of his spiritual children gathered to mourn around his bier. Just before the coffin was lowered into the vault, Rev Daniel Rogers of Exeter offered a prayer, during which he cried out, "O my father, my father!" when overwhelmed by his own emotions. He sat down and wept aloud, while sighs and sobs came from every part of the church; and as the great congregation broke up, people went to their homes weeping silently. The sad tidings of his death reached London November 5, 1770.

"Whitefield was the prince of English preachers," says an English critic. "Many have surpassed him as sermon-makers, but none have approached him as a pulpit orator. Many have outshone him in the clarity of their logic, the grandeur of their conception, and the sparkling beauty of single sentences; but in the power of darting the gospel direct into the conscience, he eclipsed them all.

"He was an orator, but he only sought to be an evangelist. Indeed, so simple was his nature, that glory to God and good-will to men having filled it, there was room for little more. Having no church to found, no family to enrich, and no memory to immortalise, he was the mere ambassador of God; and inspired with its genial, piteous spirit – so full of heaven reconciled and humanity restored – he soon himself became a living gospel. Radiant with its benignity and trembling with its tenderness, by a sort of spiritual induction a vast audience would speedily be brought into a frame of mind, the transfusing of his own; and the white furrows on their sooty faces told that Kingswood colliers were weeping, or the quivering of an ostrich plume bespoke its elegant wearer's deep emotion. Coming to his work direct from communion with his Master, and in all the strength of accepted prayer, there was an elevation in his views which often paralysed hostility, and a self-possession which only made him, amid uproar and fury, the more sublime. And when it is known that his voice could be heard by twenty thousand, and that ranging all the empire, as well as America, he would often preach thrice on a working-day, and that he has received in one week as many as a thousand letters from persons awakened by his sermons, if no estimate can be formed of the results of his ministry, some idea may be suggested of its vast extent and singular effectiveness."

We have followed him for the most part in the light of his triumphs, we have listened only to the pleasant voices of those who loved him, and have heard only the echo of his soul-stirring eloquence, yet Whitefield had many foes, who made "no small stir" against him. Cowper tells us, in the beautiful tribute which he paid to his memory, how the preacher and the world quit scores; for,

> "Assailed by scandal and the tongue of strife,
> His only answer was a blameless life;
> And he that forged, and he that threw the dart,
> Had each a brother's interest in his heart.
> Paul's love of Christ, and steadiness unbribed,
> Were copied close in him, and well transcribed.
> He followed Paul – his zeal a kindred flame,
> His apostolic charity the same;
> Like him, crossed cheerfully tempestuous seas,
> Forsaking country, kindred, friends, and ease;
> Like him he laboured, and like him, content
> To bear it, suffered shame where'er he went."

Whitefield died at the age of fifty-six. He was married in 1741, but enjoyed little of domestic life, for his field was the world: one son, the only fruit of this union, was removed in early childhood, and his wife died two years before himself.

By Whitefield's will it was found that the orphan-house in Bethesda, and likewise all his buildings, land, books, and furniture in the province of Georgia, were bequeathed, as the will ran, "to that lady elect, that mother in Israel, that mirror of true and undefiled religion, the Right Honourable Selina Countess Dowager of Huntingdon;" and in case she should be called to enter upon her glorious rest before his decease, to Honourable James Habersham, a merchant of Savannah, and one also of the original Oxford band.

In a codicil appended to the will, we find a record of cherished friendships. "I also leave a mourning-ring to my honoured and dear friends the Rev John and Charles Wesley, in token of my indissoluble union with them in heart and Christian affection, notwithstanding our difference in judgment about some particular points of doctrine."

With these possessions was bequeathed to Lady Huntingdon a large revenue of care and anxiety, which, with grief for the loss of so well-beloved a friend and faithful a coadjutor, so pressed upon her spirit, that she appointed Tuesday, the 15th of January, a day of especial prayer throughout the chapels under her patronage, that the great Head of the church would pour out his Spirit both upon ministers and people, and that she herself might lay hold with a more simple and relying faith upon the "arm of the Lord," which alone is strength and protection.

Not daunted by this accession to her labours, Lady Huntingdon soon began to act with her characteristic energy. She took every measure to make herself thoroughly acquainted with the real state of the institution, which at that time contained "sixteen children, nine managers and carpenters, and seventy-five Negroes." New plans were made for its management; her own housekeeper was sent out to regulate its domestic economy; Rev Mr Crosse was appointed teacher of the school, and Mr Piercy made president and general agent of her affairs there. Meanwhile, a mission to North America was projected, whose headquarters should be at Bethesda, from which the missionaries could go forth either to the savages in the forest, or among the white men of the colonies, wherever the providence of God opened a way to publish the everlasting gospel.

Lady Huntingdon addressed a letter to all the ministers and students in her connection, inviting them to a general meeting at Trevecca, in order to consult together and to ask counsel from on high upon a measure at once so new and so important. The occasion proved to be one of unusual interest. Missionary zeal was kindled; the baptism of a self-sacrificing love fell upon many hearts; and at the call, "Who will go for us? who will publish the glad tidings of great good in the forests and frontiers of the New World?" the response came from many a youth, "Here am I, send me."

The impressive services which attended the selection and the setting apart of the students for the North American mission, both at Trevecca and Tottenham Court chapel, and in the open air on Tower Hill, were witnessed by large numbers deeply and tenderly excited by the scene.

"In October, the missionaries embarked on board a vessel destined to convey them to America, and sailed from Blackwall to Gravesend. As the moment of their departure approached," says one, "the prayers of thousands who felt themselves peculiarly interested in the arduous, yet glorious undertaking, became more frequent and fervent. Vast multitudes attended them to the river's side, and as soon as the boats conveyed them from the shore, every countenance was suffused with tears, hats and handkerchiefs were seen waving in every direction, while prayers and wishes ascended like a cloud of incense to the great Head of the church, commending them to his merciful protection and guardian care. Such a spirit of prayer and supplication was poured out upon the people of God at this interesting period, as has seldom been remembered."

The vessel being detained in the downs by adverse winds, the missionaries had several opportunities of going on shore, which they gladly improved, preaching with the fervour of men who had given their all to the service of their Lord, and setting the current of pious sympathy strongly in favour of the missionary enterprise. "Nor was anything so blessed," said Lady Huntingdon, "as the spirit in which they went."

After a six weeks' voyage, the company arrived safely in Georgia, where they met with a cordial reception from Whitefield's friends; the orphan-house became their head-quarters, and never, perhaps, did so many favourable circumstances seem to conspire to the happy furtherance of missionary labour.

"The province of Georgia," Lady Huntingdon tells us, "have made proposals to build a church at their own expense and present me with it, that the college of Georgia may have their ministry in that part honoured. My last letters from America inform me, that our way seems open to the Cherokee country; and in all the back settlements we are assured the people will joyfully build us churches at their own expense, and present them to us, to settle perpetually for our use. Some great, very great work is intended by the Lord among the heathen. Should this appear, I should be rejoiced to go myself and establish a college for the Indian nations. I cannot help thinking that the Lord will have me there before I die, if only to make coats and garments for the poor Indians."

Thus hopefully begun was this enterprise, thus broad and buoyant were the expectations which fanned the ardour and guided the strength of her who stood at its helm, watching with a keen eye, a reverent and earnest spirit, the progress of her richly freighted argosy.

In the midst of these bright hopes, tidings reached England of the destruction of the orphan-house by fire. The loss was great, and so we may suppose must have been the disappointment; and yet what does Lady Huntingdon say: "Though we may be disappointed, God the judge of all is not defeated; all things are ordered according to the counsel of his own will; I cannot wish it for one moment to be otherwise."

From all that can be gathered, Lady Huntingdon's temporal affairs in Georgia seem not to have been well managed. For several years she spent large sums with few cheering results. The breaking out of the revolutionary war threw everything into disorder; Piercy returned to England, and in 1782 the estates were seized by the Americans, though she says her greatest losses were by the king's troops. Collisions with the state authorities afterwards occurred, and the establishment for orphans passed away. Thus closed the career of an institution which was the cherished favourite of the religious public a hundred years ago.

The actual amount of good accomplished by the associations and institutions of pious men for human renovation, cannot always be measured by their outlays, or their permanency. They are intended to bear upon the spiritual kingdom of our Lord; and how many consciences have been pierced, how many burdens removed, how many souls saved, how many prayers elicited, how much love kindled, how much covetousness rebuked, how much unbelief chastised, how much sloth removed, in a word, *how much training for eternity* has been accomplished through their instrumentality, we can never fully know this side of the grave. The direct object of their projectors may not have been as completely answered as seemed desirable; no large revenue of positive usefulness may have been palpably gathered in, and to the worldly looker-on only disappointment and defeat may seem to reward our utmost painstaking. But the aspect of affairs is quite different viewed from the Christian standpoint. Here we learn, that the one vital interest of each one of us is, to do God's will and grow into his likeness; that it is the hearty and humble desire to glorify God in whatever we do, and not the success which may crown *our* efforts, which becomes the true measure of a well-spent life.

We may rejoice and be thankful when God honours us by making us the instruments of doing great things for his kingdom here below; but we need not be cast down when, by his providence, he sees fit to break in upon our most cherished plans for good. He knows better than we what springs to touch and what wheels to turn in the mighty machinery of his moral government. He knows also what ordering is best to fit us for heaven; and the humble and trusting spirit, a heart patiently waiting and loving its Saviour's will upon a sick-bed, may constitute a more perfected life, than many a one whose deeds ring round the world.

16

Venn Leaving Huddersfield – Labours of Lady Huntingdon – Death of Howell Harris and Lord Chesterfield

M R VENN had now been settled twelve years in Huddersfield, and had made full proof of a blessed ministry, not only to the people of his particular charge, but to many a neighbouring hamlet and cotter's home.

The pastoral labours of this excellent man were everywhere attended with marked success; and it is a question of no common interest, in these times of spiritual barrenness, what was the secret of his success, or what the gifts and graces which secured to him so fast a hold upon the consciences and affections of his hearers.

"Look upon your people," he said to his son John, on entering upon the sacred office, "as prisoners under condemnation, for whose pardon and recovery you ought to feel as the tender mother does for the child at her breast. Lament an unfeeling heart in yourself as well as in them; beg earnestly that you may long after their salvation in the bowels of the Lord Jesus Christ." And he regarded as a qualification of the ministry more necessary almost than any other, "a deep sense of your own unworthiness – necessary to make you speak with consciousness of your poverty and ignorance; necessary to teach you how to speak to the weary and tempted soul; necessary to lay hold on Christ, and find in him more than all you need, for acceptance, strength, comfort, and usefulness; and necessary to make you take pains, and give yourself wholly to the work, that your profiting may appear;" nor can we doubt that this was the transcript of his own experience, leading him to those labours of love which distinguished and adorned his life.

Let us go now among the people, and hear what mention they make of their pastor and preacher.

"There was a meeting every Saturday night of the most pious people at Thomas Hanson's, sometimes twenty or more, who sang and prayed together," an old parishioner goes on to say; "and I was first led to the Huddersfield church by listening with an uncle of mine at the door of the house where the meeting was held. We thought there was something uncommon to make them so earnest, so we went together to the church one Thursday evening. There was a great crowd within the church all silent, many weeping. The text was, 'Thou art laid in the balances, and art found wanting.' When we got out of church, we did not say a word to each other till we got some way into the fields. Then my uncle stopped, leaned his back against a wall, and burst into tears, crying out, 'I can't stand this.' His convictions of sin from that time were most powerful, and he became quite a changed character, and a most exemplary person, as people will testify. After that sermon I could no longer be easy in sin. I began to pray earnestly, and soon to seek salvation in earnest. The people used to go from Longwood in droves to Huddersfield church, three miles off; scores of them came out of church together, whose ways home were in this direction, and they used to stop at the Firs' End, a mile off, and talk over for some time what they had heard. O, that place has been to me like a little heaven below. Never was a minister like our minister. He was most powerful in unfolding the terrors of the law; when doing so, he had a stern look that would make you tremble: then he would turn off to the offers of grace, and begin to smile, and go on entreating till his eyes filled with tears. The most wicked and ill-conditioned men went to hear him, and they fell like slaked lime, in a moment."

"Always at work," adds another, "he took every method of instructing his people, he left nothing unturned. The lads he catechised used to tell him that people said he was teaching a new doctrine, and leading them into error; but he always replied, 'Never mind them, do not answer them; read your Bibles and press forward, dear lads, press forward, and you cannot miss of heaven.'

"Everywhere were the fruits of his ministry. Sinners were reclaimed, children were trained in the fear of God, piety was quickened, numbers were added to the people of God, the stated means of grace were diligently improved, a saving and healthy influence went forth from the church, and as a consequence, the Sabbath was respected, sobriety prevailed, scoffing and infidelity were rebuked, and good morals began to creep in among the ale-shops."

Mr Venn was nearly fifty, and in the prime of his usefulness; but a tendency to consumption began gradually to be developed, warning him to curtail his labours, if not altogether to desist from them; yet this was almost impossible in a parish as large as that of Huddersfield. A summer journey did not materially benefit him, although we find him preaching here and there by the way. Tarrying a while at Lady Huntingdon's hospitable mansion at Bath, the mournful tidings of Mr Whitefield's death reached England, and he undertook the sad and solemn task of preaching a funeral-sermon at the Bath chapel, now bereft of one of its strong pillars.

It was during this visit that Mr Venn received an offer of the curacy of Yelling, a small town about twelve miles from Cambridge, and every consideration of prudence urged him to accept it. But to leave Huddersfield, to part from the "dearly loved and longed for, his joy and crown," the thought was deeply afflicting; and when he accepted Yelling, and the decision was known at Huddersfield, never were witnessed sadder scenes on a like occasion. "How can we let thee go?" was the universal cry, and they almost constrained him to tarry with them. During the three months preceding his removal, so many and so affecting were the tokens of his people's love, that Mr Venn was in a strait betwixt two; and when he preached his farewell sermon, people flocked from all parts to hear him, and weeping mothers held up their children, saying, "There is the man who has been our most faithful minister, and our best friend."

"No human being," wrote Venn to Lady Huntingdon, "can tell how keenly I feel this separation from a people I have so dearly loved; your ladyship well knows how much I am attached to Huddersfield, where my poor labours have been acknowledged by the great Lord of the harvest, and where I have enjoyed so much and such near communion and fellowship with the Father and his Son Jesus Christ; but the shattered state of my health incapacitates me for the care of so large a parish. And now, my dear lady, my most faithful friend, pray for me, that the blessing of the Lord our God may go with me, and render my feeble attempts to speak of his love and mercy efficacious to the conversion of souls. At Yelling, as at

Huddersfield, I shall still be your ladyship's willing servant in the service of the gospel; and when I can be of any service in furthering your plans for the salvation of souls and the glory of Christ, I am your obedient servant to command."

The parish of Yelling was thinly inhabited, and a congregation of twenty or thirty rustics wore a very different aspect from the large and intelligently trained audience which he used to preach to; "but they are remarkably attentive," he writes to Lady Huntingdon, "and seem to wonder very much at my doctrine and earnest manner. Dear Mr Berridge has been here, and has preached for me. He encourages me to go into the neighbouring parishes, where he has preached occasionally, and I have already had several congregations in barns and other places, where I hope good has been done. Your ladyship would enjoy the sight of one of these rustic assemblies, and the avidity with which they drink in, as it were, every expression that falls from my lips.

Souls are perishing in every direction around me, but I have not strength to go forth as I once did. I long to see your ladyship, and to hear once more the many precious things from your lips which invigorated my dead soul, and gave me such vehement desires in times past. Oh, pray that I may be animated with a burning desire to spread the glorious gospel of my precious Lord and Master, and be content to spend and be spent in a cause so divine."

We are left in no doubt what it was that gave such transforming power to the pastoral ministrations of this man of God. He *felt the truth and reality of redemption.* "What an unspeakable mercy," he exclaims with admiring gratitude, "to be rescued from the bondage of sin, to enjoy the presence of God, to behold the glory of God, to feel his support, his protection, and his victorious arm stretched out on our behalf; and thus to *walk with him on earth,* and endure as seeing Him who is invisible. This is a hard work – at least, I find it so; but this is our *daily business,* together with that of our particular calling. Against this walk with our God, the company of three armies as it were, the world, the flesh, and Satan, fight continually; but let us not be discouraged, for this is our consolation: 'The Lord will give strength unto his people; the Lord will bless his people with peace.'" Is not the life of such a man a fresh witness of the power and excellency of divine truth? Mr Venn removed to Yelling in 1771.

Meanwhile the unquenchable zeal of Lady Huntingdon found many outlets through the labours of her students, who now began to traverse every part of the kingdom, bravely and vigilantly carrying on a guerrilla warfare with the powers of sin and Satan. They went into the highways and hedges, preaching and teaching with apostolic fidelity, and whenever the weather was favourable "using a table for a pulpit and the canopy of the heavens for a sounding-board, and ever beseeching the Lord Jesus to preside over their assemblies."

"And it seems to be the prevailing spirit of the present students to do this everywhere," Lady Huntingdon tells us; "the gift of awakening seems much continued to our plan and work; the spread is astonishing; the college does not yet fill equal to our calls, but the fewer the more useful: they appear like Gideon's army."

At one time we hear of a congregation of fifteen hundred poor colliers and nailers. At another, of ten thousand in a large, deep hollow; and Lady Huntingdon herself is at Cornwall, saying, "My call here is to the tinners, and thousands and tens of thousands of poor perishing creatures, who all seem to neglect their souls, are the object of my loving care. If the Lord permit, I wish to make three or four establishments in the heart of the tin mines, for their instruction and salvation."

She passed much time at Trevecca, her "beloved retreat," as she called it, secluded as it was from the clamour and strife of the world, yet animated with the generous impulses and devotional ardour of a band of pious youth, ready, through evil and through good report, to bear witness for their Lord. Here she maintained an extensive correspondence with her numerous friends, preachers, and various people connected by business with her different departments of religious effort. Indeed, the management of her business required the time, attention, and energy of no common man; and yet she entered into its details and encountered its perplexities with a courage and patience which neither age nor infirmities could long damp, and which they could never destroy.

We now find her travelling in different counties, following up with her presence the labours of her missionaries, inspecting her chapels, investigating the doings of trustees and committees, regulating salaries, directing funds, counselling, controlling, and encouraging, with an unspent force of mind which was marvellous to behold.

A letter to one of her committees having the charge of a chapel, may serve to show the kind and amount of her labours, as well as the faith which sustained her amid the greatest discouragements and perplexities.

"My WORTHY FRIENDS – You must allow me to assure you that the pleasure I had in reading the conclusion of your letter did abundantly outweigh those many complaints, and I hope needless fears, which our gracious Lord is forced to try us by, and *that* in order that we may see the only hand worthy to expect our blessing from, and yield him all the praise. More I want not, than to find our Lord own our assemblies as *his*. No good thing shall be withheld while the Lord of hosts remains the tender Father of us his Israel, and will afford us our meat in due season.

"I lament a complaint should come on Mr Taylor's account, and have sent a direction to provide for him from my own property, as no collection can be had at Tunbridge Wells, owing to the great poverty of the people. The income of an estate of mine has ever been freely given to support the gospel in that part of Kent, with an allowance for the winter food of a student, as no minister can pay this out of what is received. Mr Taylor cannot have more for his support for four months there, than is allowed through all the churches; and in case of his absence, a minister is to be boarded by him, as is the student, supported in part by the people, all the winter. The purpose that is intended bears no proportion of difficulty to me, who only am the responsible person for the debts and deficiencies that may arise on the chapel. I am still willing to trust my dear and faithful Master; he has ever dealt kindly by his poor old worthless servant, and I do not find that I want a better bank to maintain food and raiment for me, or those proper and just supplies he shall afford for his various little households, which he orders or may order for my ignorant care of them. As to the minister's board, your allowance of two guineas a week just comes to what you have stated.

"As to a reader, we have no such example among us. The Gardens have one for the sake of the prayers when a student preaches, but no one minister has ever had a single difficulty; and it appears to me, allowing the minister ten guineas who stays a quarter with you, to find a reader if he likes, will be less expense than the burden of regularly maintaining one. Many choose to read the prayers, and I must say the air of superiority and importance thus manifested has not that simplicity that means neither show or parade. The more apostolic we are the better; and I must say, as a most remarkable blessing, I know of none anxious or discontented among us, even when it might have been justly excused, seeing myself unable to do what my heart so much desired. My best advice to you is, to be wisely cautious upon this point; and either collections or private subscriptions from honest and devoted hearts, privately applied to for this purpose, as a little loan to the Lord, and not necessity, will go further to bless such means than the many affected shows supposed liberality wears. I am sure you expect a faithful answer from me, and 'such as I have, give I unto you' all. Do not be careful about the household stuff; my dear Master will not let me want table or chairs. You see where all my cares are cast. Commending your gracious labours to Him whose faithful and tender eye is ever over you, I remain, my worthy friends, your faithful, willing, and ever ready friend and devoted servant,

"S. HUNTINGDON"

This was addressed to the committee of one of her London chapels, several of which she had erected or hired for the accommodation of the poorer flocks, who without them had been as sheep without a shepherd.

The second of her London efforts was the renting of a large building in Princes Street, Westminster, which she repaired and enlarged, with the aid willingly rendered to her by some of her wealthy friends interested in the Redeemer's kingdom. For some time this chapel was supplied by ministers from the established church, among whom we find the name of Toplady, a name familiar to the lovers of lyrical poetry. "The congregation is very numerous," she tells us, "and many of the mighty and noble, as well as the poor, gladly hear the Word, to some of whom it has proved the savour of life."

The next in succession was the Mulberry Gardens chapel, fitted up in a tasteful and elegant manner, and opened according to the forms of the Church of England. The labours of its ministers gave great offence to many in the neighbourhood, who, alarmed at their popularity, and shamed by their diligence, endeavoured to silence them by various acts of persecution. These efforts were fruitless; great success attended their ministrations, owned and blessed as they were by the great Head of the church.

In 1773, Lady Huntingdon lost two friends with whom she had been long and differently associated. "That indefatigable servant of God, Howell Harris, fell asleep in Jesus last week," she writes to Romaine. "When he was confined to his bed, and could no longer preach or exhort, he said, 'Blessed be God, my work is done, and I know that I am going to my God and Father, for he hath my heart, yea, my whole heart. Glory be to God, death hath no sting – all is well;' and thus this good man went home to his rest.

"It is impossible to describe the grief which is awakened everywhere by the tidings of his death, he was so beloved as the spiritual father of multitudes. Truly his loss is felt at the college, where many were awakened by his lively ministry. The last time he preached at college, he spoke with a mighty sense of God, eternity, and immortality; and when he came to the application, he addressed himself to the audience in such a tender, earnest, and moving manner, exhorting us to come and be acquainted with the dear Redeemer, as melted the assembly into tears.

"On the day of his interment, we had some special seasons of divine influence, both upon converted and unconverted. No fewer than twenty thousand persons were assembled, and we had abundance of students in the college, and all the ministers and exhorters, who collected from various parts to pay their last tribute to his remains. We had three stages erected, and nine sermons addressed to the vast multitudes, hundreds of whom were dissolved in tears. Fifteen clergymen were present, six of whom blew the gospel trumpet with great power and freedom. Though we had enjoyed much of the gracious presence of God in our assemblies before, yet I never saw so much at any one time as on that day, especially when the Lord's Supper was administered, God poured out his Spirit in a wonderful manner. Many old Christians told me they never had seen so much of the glory of the Lord and the riches of his grace, nor felt so much of the power of the gospel before. I hope soon to open a chapel in Worcester. Lincolnshire and Kent promise great things. Lady Fanny Shirley has frequent meetings at her house in Bath, where the nobility attend. The work spreads amazingly in Gloucestershire.

"When you have a little leisure, Mr Shirley will be glad of your assistance in Brighton, Mr Venn is now at Oathall. I expect here, in a month, also Mr Toplady and Mr Berridge."

In contrast with the death of Howell Harris stands that of Lord Chesterfield, which occurred a few months afterwards. He had been the early friend and companion of Earl Huntingdon; after whose death, he seems always to have remained on a friendly footing with the countess. Towards the young earl we find him acting as towards an adopted son, a circumstance which Lady Huntingdon is presumed not to have been able to control, and which must have occasioned her no little sorrow.

His scepticism and profligacy did not prevent him from frequently attending on the ministrations of Whitefield, whose eloquence he greatly admired, and at Lady Huntingdon's solicitations, he often contributed to the cause of Christ.

"Really there is no resisting your ladyship's importunities," he once replied to her: "It would ill become me to censure your enthusiastic admiration of Mr Whitefield; his eloquence is unrivalled, his zeal inexhaustible, and not to admire both would argue a total absence of taste, and an insensibility not to be coveted by anybody. Your ladyship is a powerful auxiliary to the Methodist cabinet; and I confess, notwithstanding my own private feelings and sentiments, I am infinitely pleased at your zeal in so good a cause. You must have twenty pounds for this new tabernacle, but I must *beg my name not to appear in any way.*"

And it was unto him according to his desires; his name was never enrolled among those who loved their Lord, while his corrupt principles and maxims are handed down to us in a volume of "*Letters to his Son*," a book which illustrates the well-known, yet often to be repeated lesson, that bright talents can make no amends for bad morals. "Death," he declared to be "a leap in the dark," and dark and dreadful did he find the leap to be. As the pains of dissolving nature increased upon him, and human help was vain, his cold and mocking scepticism could offer neither present alleviations nor future hope. "The blackness of darkness, accompanied by every gloomy horror, thickened most awfully around his dying moments," says Lady Huntingdon, who vainly tried to administer the only consolation which could avail.

Far different was the impression which Lady Fanny Shirley on her sick-bed made upon the surrounding attendants. Once, as a reigning beauty at court, Chesterfield had addressed to her some of his most famous epigrams; since then, she had chosen that better part which could never be taken from her.

"I am quite at a loss to explain how Lady Fanny is enabled to bear such a severity of suffering with so much tranquillity, and so few symptoms of restlessness and murmuring," said her physician to Mr Venn; "can you account for it, sir?"

"Sir," answered Venn, "that lady happily possesses what you and I ought daily to pray for, the grace of her Lord Jesus Christ, the love of God, and the fellowship of the Holy Ghost." What supports are these! After Lord Chesterfield's death, Rowland Hill became chaplain to his lady.

In the early part of the year 1775, Lady Huntingdon is at Bath, preparing for the opening of her chapel in Bristol. "Opening a chapel in Chichester, with the business which arises from the amazing increase of our work, allows me little time to indulge myself even in that of more constant intercourse with my friends," she says, and we may well conclude she allows no hindrances to stop her, for four new chapels are opened this year in different parts of the kingdom.

Some misunderstanding having arisen between Lady Huntingdon and the trustees of the Tabernacle, Berridge, on his annual visit to the metropolis, inquired into its origin, and thus discourses to her ladyship:

"My DEAR LADY – Mrs Carteret tells me I owe you a letter, and your ladyship might tell Mrs Carteret I owe you much love, which will ever be paying, I trust, and never be paid. Demands on this score, if honestly made, are always welcome; and if roguishly practised, are quickly forgiven. For who ever thought of hanging a *love thief*, except a disappointed lover? A miser, who cannot open the string of his purse without pain, can part with the string of his heart freely to a bountiful friend; and the favours you have shown me call out for more than one heartstring – a dozen, at least.

"'Well, well, enough of this,' you say; 'but what have you seen or heard at London? As you are an old fellow with a prattling tongue, I shall expect a long history, but let it be a faithful one.' Indeed, my Lady, I have seen and heard some things to please me, and some things to grieve me. I have seen the Tabernacle temple well crowded with attentive hearers, which has cheered my heart; but the Tabernacle house deserted by your students, which has grieved my spirit. Upon asking the cause, I was told the trustees were suspected of a design on your Mulberry Gardens. What has occasioned that suspicion I know not, but I well know they had no more desire to steal your *mulberries,* than to steal my *teeth;* and I believe the *profit* of the mulberries, if that base thing had been in view, would no more enable them to buy a crust, than my old teeth would enable them to bite it. When the yearly accounts of the two chapels are made up, I know they are sometimes below par, and have seldom £20 in hand; and the Mulberry Gardens, if under their management, were not likely to produce any other gain besides trouble. Indeed, my Lady, I am well satisfied that the trustees have been your hearty friends and faithful servants, and am sorry to find they are much offended at your suspicions. Could I discern lucrative views in them, as much as I love the Tabernacle – that old beehive, which has filled many hives with her swarms – I would visit her no longer. But the more I know of the trustees, the more I am confirmed of their integrity, which they will give a proof of shortly by adopting Dr Ford as a third trustee.

"Well, now I am prattling, I must even prattle on; an old man's tongue is like a 'larum – when it sets off, though teasing enough, it will run down. But you cry, 'No more griefs, pray, Mr Grievous, unless you intend to set me a yawning.' Indeed, my Lady, I have another, and beg you would seal up your lips to prevent yawning, if that is indecent out of a church. I am told, and simply tell you my tale, that since the trustees were dismissed from your service, you have taken a Tory ministry, are growing sadly churchified, and seem to walk with a steeple on your head, newly sprung up, but pointing very high. As to the steeple, I heed it not; a smart heavenly breeze will soon blow that down; but I cannot be reconciled, like some of my brethren, to a Tory ministry and a church-wall spirit. I regard neither high-church nor low-church, nor any church but the church of Christ, which is not built with hands, nor circumscribed within peculiar walls, nor confined to a singular denomination. I cordially approve the doctrines and liturgy of the Church of England, and have cause to bless God for a church house to preach in, and a church revenue to live on. And I could wish the gospel might not only be preached in all the British churches, but established therein by Christ's Spirit, as well as by a national statute; but from the principles of the clergy and the leading men in the nation, which are growing continually more unscriptural and licentious, I do fear our defence is departing, and the glory is removing from our Israel. Perhaps in less than one hundred years to come the church lands may be seized on to hedge up government gaps, as the abbey lands were two hundred and fifty years ago.

"But you say the Lord is sending many gospel labourers into the church. True; and with a view, I think, of calling his people out of it. Because, when such ministers are removed by death, or transported to another vineyard, I see no fresh gospel labourer succeed them, which obliges the forsaken flocks to fly to a meeting. And what else can they do? If they have tasted of manna and hunger for it, they cannot feed on heathen chaff, nor yet on legal crusts, though baked by some staunch Pharisee quite up to perfection. What has become of Mr Venn's Yorkshire flock, what will become of his Yelling flock, or of my flocks, at our decease? Or what will become of your students at your removal? They are virtual dissenters now, and will be settled dissenters then. And the same will happen to many, perhaps most of Mr Wesley's preachers, at his death. He rules like a real Alexander, and is now stepping forth with a flaming torch; but we do not read in history of two Alexander's succeeding each other.

"But you reply, 'Some of my best preachers leave me in my life-time.' Perhaps they may; and if I may judge of your feelings by my own on such occasions, this must grieve you, on the first view at least; but wait and see whether the Lord's hand be not in it. I dare not commend Barnabas for his abrupt departure from Paul; yet it might be permitted, with a view of sending him to Cyprus. The Lord can, and often does make the wrath of man, or the foolishness of man, turn to his praise. However, it is good for us, I know, to have our well-meant views frequently perplexed and overturned, else we might grow headstrong, and fancy ourselves wise enough to be the Lord's privy-councillors, yea, able to out-counsel him. We had rather sit with Jesus at the council-board than follow him with a string on our nose, to turn us round, or turn us back, at his pleasure. Some years ago, two of my lay-preachers deserted their ranks and joined the dissenters. This threw me into a violent fit of the spleen, and set me a coughing and barking exceedingly; but when the phlegm was come up, and leisure allowed for calm thought, I did humbly con-ceive the Lord Jesus might be wiser than the old vicar, and did well in sending some preachers from the Methodist mint among the dissenters, to revive a drooping cause, and set old crippled pilgrims on their legs again. Nay, it is certain that some of these deserting preachers have not only quickened the Chelsea invalids, but raised up new and vigorous recruits for the King's service. Be glad, therefore, my Lady, to promote the Lord's cause in any way – in your own line, if it may be; in another line, if it must be. If your preachers abide with you and are valiant for the truth, it is well; if they depart, let them depart, and rejoice that you have been instrumental in sending them forth. If a lively preacher goes, he will prove a live coal among dying embers; if a dead one departs, he is buried out of your sight.

"Paul tells me in one place, 'All in Asia are turned aside from me;' and in another, he says, 'Some preached Christ out of envy and strife,' out of envy and opposition to him; yet he adds, 'What then? Every way Christ is preached; and therein I do rejoice, yea, and will rejoice.' Here is a pattern for our imitation. However rusty or rickety the dissenters may appear to you, God hath his remnant among them; therefore lift not up your hand against them for the Lord's sake, nor yet for consistency's sake, because your students are as real dissenting preachers as any in the land, unless a gown and band can make a clergyman. The bishops look on your students as the worst kind of dissenters; and manifest this by refusing that ordination to your preachers which would be readily granted to other teachers among the dissenters.

"When I consider that the doctrines of grace are a common offence to the clergy, and the Bible itself a fulsome nuisance to the great vulgar – that powerful efforts have been made to eject the gospel doctrines out of the church, and the likelihood there is, from the nation's infidelity, of a future attempt succeeding, there is room to fear, when the church doctrines are banished from the church by a national act, Jesus will utterly remove the candlestick, and take away his church bread from those hirelings who eat it and lift up the heel against him.

"So you are whispering to Lady Anne, 'This old vicar is very tedious, and growing pedantic too. He would fain turn a seer, and has not wit enough for a common conjurer or a strolling fortune-teller; but he is often eaten up with the vapours, poor man, and I must excuse him.' Indeed, I am not *wholly* eaten up with the vapours, and cannot be, because I am much eaten up aforehand with esteem for your Ladyship. I know your zeal for the Master's honour, and for the prosperity of his Zion, which must endear you to every honest hearted pilgrim. The good Shepherd be your guide and guard; may his cloud direct all your motions, and distil a gracious dew upon yourself, and upon your students. Please do present my respects to Lady Anne and Miss Orton; and believe me to remain your hearty well-wisher and affectionate servant,

   "JOHN BERRIDGE"

17
The Rectory of Yelling

HITHERTO we have been occupied chiefly with the public labours of these servants of God in the Great Awakening. Scepticism had fled away before the keen edge of the truths which they wielded, and mere nominal Christianity acknowledged its weakness; while vice and degradation had yielded to the only power which could heal and save. But there was something in their influence more positive still: everywhere their presence infused a new and holier life, whose gentle charities distilled like dew upon English homes, endearing the tie of husband and wife, parents and children, and making the family a household of faith, "abounding in love towards one another, and towards all men." Let us behold these fruits of piety as they grow in "social sweetness" in the rectory of Yelling.

At the time of his removal from Huddersfield, Mr Venn was a widower with five children, the eldest of whom was but thirteen. Soon afterwards, he formed an engagement with an old and valued friend, to whom he thus wrote shortly before their marriage.

"Long was I very backward to think of entering again into the married state, though so blessed in my first connection; but the gracious God whom I serve, and whose I am, has provided for me one of his own elect. I begin to feel more concern than I at first did, lest my children should give you trouble; for just in the same proportion as I love and value you, I must feel anything that in any degree may affect you. And I say to myself, 'How should I be able to bear seeing my dear wife in tears, or void of her sweet cheerfulness and vivacity of spirit by any of my children, to whom she has so kindly shown herself a friend indeed.' I hope it will not be so; and if prayer can avail to prevent such a trial coming upon her, she will never experience any sorrow on my account, or those belonging to me, but by our departure.

"You may remember how pleasantly you said Hogarth would describe our courtship. In what light would the world regard my letters? Strange love-letters indeed! O, did they but know how much more blessed are the faithful in Christ, in every relation of life, than themselves, the love of present enjoyment would make them converts to the faith. But all this is hid from their eyes. They cannot understand how a solid acquaintance with a crucified Saviour diffuses an influence through the whole life, and renders the husband, the wife, the father, the master, the servant, the child, the friend a very different creature, and far more excellent than what he would otherwise be."

At the marriage his scattered household reassembled around him, and he exclaims, "We are all now under one roof. Important and awful connection; which I wish and pray may be more and more imprinted upon my mind. How contrary to nature, to consider our nearest relatives in this light, and to say often and solemnly, my father or mother, husband or wife, children or servants are the very persons with whom, as I have the most to do, so shall I have the most to answer for. With what circumspection, with what zeal, with what tenderness of love, should we do good, and edify and comfort one another."

Mr Venn accepted Yelling as a "providential retreat," where, though shattered in health, he might scatter a few more seeds, and gather a little harvest for the Lord of glory; but if not rest, freedom from the manifold cares and excitements of a large parish, seems to have been just what he most needed. His health gradually improved, and the strength he was praying for, for so many years before he left Yorkshire, was vouchsafed to him at Yelling.

"Week after week passes," he says again, "and except on a Sunday, we see nothing but trees and sheep, and a pheasant or two passing over the field; yet I am quite joyous, and solitude is to the full as delicious as it used to be twenty years ago at Clapham; yet as the Swiss have a certain longing which comes over them at times to see their own country again, I feel something of this towards Huddersfield."

"You tell me you have no idea how we go on," he writes to a friend. "Take the following sketch: I am up, one of the first in the house, soon after five; and when prayer and reading the blessed Word is done, my daughters make their appearance, and I teach them until Mrs Venn comes down at half past eight. Then family prayer begins, which is often very sweet, as my mother's maid and my own servants are, I believe, born of God. The children begin to sing prettily, and our praises, I trust, are heard on high. From breakfast, we are all employed till we ride out, in fine weather, two hours for health; and after dinner, employed again. At six, I have always one hour for solemn meditation and walking in my house or the church till seven. We have then, sometimes twenty, sometimes more or less of the people, to whom I expound the Word of the blessed God: several appear much affected; and sometimes Jesus stands in the midst and saith, 'Peace be unto you.' Our devotions end at eight; we sup, and go to rest at ten. On Sundays, I am able to speak six hours at three different times, to my own great surprise. Oh, the goodness of God in raising me up."

The delights vouchsafed to the children of God, and which constitute them a "peculiar people," are strikingly exhibited when the rector of Yelling says, "I have now been here three years and three months. Take notice, never absent but eleven out of one hundred and seventy Sundays; and sometimes not a night in a month. Is not this residence? and never more pleased than when no visitor came near us, though no one delights more in the company of his friends, and the friends of Jesus.

"But I find unspeakable joy in the Word of grace, at the throne of grace, in meditation and contemplation, in recalling past marvellous mercies and distinguishing grace, in looking forward to the final scene of man's eventful history and my own pilgrimage; while the business I have with my family, and my sermons – meeting with a few poor cottagers every evening, who are, I trust, members of Christ – make each passing day glide on apace; and weeks and months and years bring with them abounding evidence of God's faithfulness and overflowing goodness and everlasting love to the vilest of the vile, as I sometimes do indeed appear to myself."

"But I have long since found, that if I turn my eyes from Jesus, and expect my comfort from anything but from himself, I must be disappointed." Such was the spirit with which he met the trials of the spiritual husbandman. "Twenty-five years ago, I was certain I could reconcile the Word of God in all its parts, and be able to pray without distraction. Now I wait for the light of eternity and the perfection of holiness, in order that I may know anything as I ought to know."

Yet he laboured lovingly on. "I have just now," he tells us, "ventured on an undertaking for the dear children of my parish. I have engaged a master to teach them all. How tenderly did our Saviour recommend little children to our regard. Had I any time to begin anew, I would give myself more to this work. In these labours of love, a sweet peace of mind is enjoyed; and when we teach, we are taught by the great Master of assemblies. I venerate the name of Dr Francke of Halle, Saxony, who, when a professor of greatest note in that university, felt his bowels yearn over the children of the poor, and became their teacher, though derided by the university for his heavenly compassion. So differently did his God regard the good work, that, from a small beginning, it was soon enlarged to be among the first charitable foundations, embalming his name for ages to come."

In 1777, his son John went to Cambridge, and was entered as a student at Sidney College. The introduction of a child on this sphere of effort, of discipline, and of temptation must needs always be an event of deep and anxious interest to the Christian parent. This son had not disappointed parental fidelity, he grew up in the fear and nurture of the Lord; and solicitous to keep the fountain pure and guard well the outposts of Christian character, the father impresses upon the lad the importance of dwelling much upon the substantial parts of a Christian's life. "This substantial part," says he, "is modesty and chastity, in opposition to pertness and impurity – temperance and sobriety, confronting the surfeit or drunkenness of epicures – humility and meekness, in opposition to natural haughtiness and angry pride – guarded cheerfulness, under a sense both of the divine presence and the mischief of noisy mirth – love to God and his Word, expressed by a stern look when scoffers pour out foolishness, and when a *double entendre* or an infidel sneer is uttered – love of diligent study, serious acquaintance, useful conversation, with secret prayer and meditation on the Word of Christ.

"Conscious that you are living thus, and that this is your earnest purpose and daily prayer, you need have no fear that you are making a compromise with the world, or want that zeal for the Lord which true faith inspires. Nothing will put to silence the ignorance of foolish men and conquer their prejudices like the humility, meekness, wisdom, and soundness of mind which those who are really in Christ possess and manifest.

"I would advise you to study with attention and exactness *their* characters who have obtained the immortal honour that they 'pleased God;' such as Enoch, Noah, Abraham, Moses, Joshua, Job. You may be sure nothing is misrepresented here. You will see what manner of persons the Spirit of God does form; you will see that supreme love to him, undaunted valour in his cause, and resignation to his will, fully possessed them. Then, lifting up your heart and eyes to their God and your God, beg that, under a more luminous dispensation and richer helps for spiritual life and godliness, you may be a follower of them who are set before you for examples."

To Eling, his eldest daughter, he thus pours out his soul in a letter on one of her birthdays: "I wish you to be saying a thousand and a thousand times to yourself, 'I am none of my own; I am the Lord's. Infinite honour, unequalled grandeur of condition, is included in this relation. May I know how to set a just value upon it. *I am the Lord's,* to have the benefit of his wisdom and unerring counsel. *I am the Lord's,* to desire from his might, ability to do those things which by nature we cannot do. *I am the Lord's,* to be preserved and defended by his tender care in this world of pits and snares and seducing objects and malignant spirits. *I am the Lord's,* to hear his voice and treasure up his divine sayings. *I am the Lord's,* to do the work he has given me to do by the allotment of his providence, and to be intent on discharging it with all diligence, humility, and cheerfulness. *I am the Lord's,* not only to live, but to die unto him.' Thus may our dear Eling be taught; and thus reckon herself to be alive to God from the dead, through Jesus Christ our Lord. This is the whole my heart can wish you. May you, living and dying, *be the Lord's.*"

"It is the pleasure and privilege peculiar to Christians to make intercession for their children," he writes to Kitty on her seventeenth birthday, "to be looking up to the Father of mercies, to bestow upon them what is necessary for their *safety,* their *comfort,* and their *usefulness.* I have therefore early in the morning of this anniversary presented my poor but sincere prayers at the throne of grace on your behalf, that you might *dwell in safety.* My dear Kitty will not be at a loss to know on what account she needs to pray herself, and to desire all that love her soul to do so too, that she may be preserved. For you know, I trust, what enemies are ever working to destroy you: your corrupt nature is your most powerful enemy. Who shall deliver you from it? He who left his throne of glory to seek and to save that which was lost. He *can* and *will,* upon your calling and lifting up your soul to him. He will create you again after his own image; give you wisdom and power to deny yourself, to do the will of God, to love him in sincerity, and to dwell in love to everyone. Then you are indeed *safe.*

"I have prayed also that you, my dear Kitty, may spend your days *in comfort* – not in show or dress, or in abundance of the things of this world, but in *solid comfort;* knowing that you are accepted of God, and that heaven is your eternal home. So our ever-blessed Saviour, when about to depart out of this world, told his dearest friends, 'I will not leave you comfortless; I will come to you. My peace I give unto you.' All desire comfort; yet young and old, rich and poor, despise or neglect Jesus of Nazareth. They cannot believe that the crucified man who died under the hands of his enemies, is the God of peace and hope; hence none in their natural state have solid comfort. One only can give it. It is pure, heart-satisfying comfort to know that you have, in the Lord of all, a companion, a counsellor, and a most familiar friend, who will be ever present with your spirit, who orders all your condition, whether you shall be sick or well, lose or still enjoy the advantage of very dear relations. In a word, this alone is comfort, to have in God a Father, to whom you can apply and rest satisfied with all his will.

"But comfort and safety are not the whole I pray the Lord to provide for your soul. *Usefulness* is the very excellency of life. No man, in the real church of Christ, liveth unto himself. Every true Christian is a tree of righteousness, whose fruits are good and profitable unto all men. He is glad to help and to comfort others. He is diligent and industrious. He dwells in peace and gentleness and love. He reproves what is wrong by an excellent example, and recommends by his own practice what is pleasing to God.

"My dear Kitty, how have you been distinguished by the divine goodness – distinguished in having your birth in a land of gospel light, in your parents being believers, in the examples you have seen, in the instructions you have received, and in the pains taken with you. All these advantages you are to improve, not as a task, but for your own enjoyment, God having inseparably connected our duty and our happiness. I figure you, therefore, to myself, as maintaining a wise, discreet, and godly conversation; satisfied with the portion the Lord divides unto his children; acquainted with spiritual blessings; filling up each day, so as to find time too short for all you have to do."

Nor did the beloved youth of his own family and parish alone share the affectionate assiduities of this devoted man. His vicinity to Cambridge brought many a serious student from college halls to the study and fireside of Yelling, where they always received a cordial welcome, and found in Mr Venn a wise counsellor and experienced teacher in heavenly things.

Mr Venn had a quick insight into character and excelled in conversation, and these rendered his social and pastoral influence very great. His manners were tender and sympathising, inspiring confidence and winning affection, and thus preparing the way for a fidelity to the immortal interests of his fellow-men which seldom gave offence. He had none of that startling, vehement, brilliant oratory which distinguished some of his illustrious associates, but his deep acquaintance with the distinguishing doctrines of the Word of God imparted an unspeakable solemnity to his manner, and a penetrating earnestness to his language; his preaching made all men feel that they had business with God and eternity which must not be trifled with, and could not be delayed.

In common with them he possessed the deep spirituality, the reverent, yet rejoicing spirit, the abasement and the elevation which distinguish those who truly walk with God. His instructions were sound, solid, and eminently practical; he aimed to establish and build up well-ordered Christian character, to foster and strengthen the habits essential to holy living.

"Every prophet and every apostle," he said to a son after he entered the ministry, "insists as much on the fruits of faith, as upon faith itself and the glory of Christ's person. The sovereign and electing grace of God, by which alone we are brought to him, bears no proportion in the Scriptures to the continued mention that is made of the absolute necessity, beauty, and excellency of a holy life and conversation – bears no proportion, I say, to the practical part of our religion." And this growth in grace, and these fruits of faith, of which

Venn himself was an eminent example, can alone spring from an experimental knowledge of, and a vital union with Christ the crucified Saviour; anything short of this is delusive, and must produce mildew, stagnation, and death.

No wonder that the young Timothys of Cambridge prized the friendship of the rector of Yelling; his influence was not lost upon them, and long after his death it was perpetuated in the godly lives of many a humble curate and zealous rector, whose devoted piety adorned the next generation of English clergymen.

18
Rowland Hill

ROWLAND HILL was now in the zenith of his popularity. Whitefield and Berridge had been his foster-fathers in the Christian life, nor did he ever disown or dishonour his spiritual birthright; with the humour of the one, and the impressive oratory of the other, united to the apostolic zeal which belonged alike to both, he appeared in the highways and by-ways of England, preaching repentance and remission of sins through Christ the crucified Saviour. In chapels and churches, market-places and moors, fields and fairs, wherever there were men to hear, there was Rowland Hill enforcing with robust earnestness that truth which thrilled his own soul; and especially were his strong sympathies drawn towards those classes where vice has no disguise, and sorrow no alleviations.

During the political riots which broke out in England in 1780, threatening the peace of the realm, he often went to St George's Fields, in the southern suburb of London, a place of disorderly assemblages and seditious vigils, and dared to address vast concourses of discontented and starving workmen upon the verities of the world to come. His intrepid addresses were charged with hidden power; they pierced the consciences of men hungry for bread, and heated with political excitement: the grievances of the present life, great as they seemed to be, and great as they really were, sank into comparative insignificance before the momentous interests of the life to come; stout hearts gave way; a cry went up for the bread of life, and they who had nothing to expect from earthly sovereigns, gained access to the throne of grace. Nor is it to be wondered at, that hatred and spite aimed their shafts at the bold yet true reformer; often he was pelted with stones, lampooned, burnt in effigy, which, with the displeasure of his parents and the undisguised uneasiness felt by many of his true yet timid friends, might have damped a heart less resolutely devoted to his Master's cause.

"True, I am what the world despises, a lay itinerant," he says, "but I am *certainly convinced* of the Lord's blessing on the work." And could he cease from it? Toplady invited him to his house in London, and tried to dissuade him from his course; but the times needed just such men, and men were raised up who recognised the call, and who were made "strong in the Lord and in the power of his might."

"Because I am in earnest," he once said at Wotton, "men call me an enthusiast. But I am not; mine are the words of truth and soberness. When I first came into this part of the country, I was walking on yonder hill; I saw a gravel-pit fall in, and bury three human beings alive. I lifted up my voice for help so loud that I was heard in the town below, at a distance of a mile; help came, and rescued two of the poor sufferers. No one called me an enthusiast then; and when I see eternal destruction ready to fall upon poor sinners, and about to entomb them irrecoverably in an eternal mass of woe, and call *aloud* on them to escape, shall I be called an enthusiast now? No, sinner, I am not an enthusiast in so doing: I call on thee aloud to fly for refuge to the hope set before thee in the gospel of Christ Jesus;" and there were times when the tremendous issues of life and death, of heaven and hell, were so vividly pictured to his own mind, that the impassioned energy of his manner was almost overwhelming. "I like to go and hear Rowland Hill," said Sheridan, "because his ideas come red-hot from the heart."

There was, indeed, no false show of feeling, no trickeries of language, no assumed oddity of manner, by which he or his illustrious compeers attracted and *riveted* the minds of both the learned and the unlearned, the rude and the refined, constraining them to honour the messages of salvation by the attentive ear, and, in how many cases, by the submission of their hearts and the renewal of their lives.

The motto of the Hill family was, "Go forward;" words of stirring significance, which Rowland had engraven on his seal, and which were the watchword and epitome of his world-known career.

"Dear sir," wrote Berridge, who marked his progress with cheerful interest, "I mean, my dear Rowley, your kind letter was long in coming, but it brought good tidings and refreshed my heart. The motto of your seal rejoiced me much; it gave me a peep into your bosom, and a taste of your letter before I read it. Indeed, I was afraid lest orders and some other things would cure you of rambling; but my fears were groundless, and all is well. The lampoon published against you is a blessed omen for good, that God intends to honour you. It seems to me a happy token that you will remain an itinerant, and that much good will arise from your ministry. Luther used to say, when the Lord had fresh work for him, a strong trial was sent beforehand to prepare him for it by humiliation. Study not to be a fine preacher. Jerichos are blown down with ram's horns. Look simply unto Jesus for preaching food; and what is wanted will be given, and what is given will be blessed, whether it be a barley or a wheaten loaf, a crust or a crumb. Your mouth will be a flowing stream, or a fountain sealed, according as your heart is. Avoid all controversy in preaching, talking, or writing; preach nothing down but the devil, and nothing up but Jesus Christ."

These irregularities finding no favour with the ecclesiastical authorities, Rowland found much difficulty in obtaining orders. His friends begged him to desist while application was being made on his behalf, and accordingly we find him at one time trying to keep quiet at the house of a pious friend in Woburn. While here, he writes to Miss Tudway, the lady whom he is about to marry, with the hearty and honest directness which always characterised him, in reply to her affectionate recommendations to abandon "the field."

"I beg you to be at ease about my conduct," he says, "since I assure you I act with all the caution in my power. I know your heart is upright before God; your fearing mind frequently perplexes you: I am sure it is a sign of a most tender heart, and such tender-hearted disciples shall never want direction from above. Here I continue a prisoner, though a prisoner at large, under this hospitable roof, and I have a hearty welcome to stay until the bishop's answer is received. On Saturday, at farthest, I shall hope to receive it, as I really dread staying over here on the Sunday, my temptations to preach will, I know, be so great; and if I do not, as I am known in these parts, I know it will slacken dear Grove's hands and grieve the dear people of God in the neighbourhood. Here as well as in other places, there seems to be a more extensive opening than ever; O that I were at liberty to labour for my God."

Through the intercession of his friends a favourable answer was received, and Rowland was at last ordained deacon by Dr Wills, the aged Bishop of Bath and Wells; and "through the kind and unexpected interposition of Providence," he says, "I was ordained without any condition or compromise whatever." It was in June, 1773.

Unfettered then by "promise or condition," the newly-made deacon having already "endured hardness as a good soldier of Jesus Christ, began to make full proof of his ministry," by again resuming his home missionary labours and preaching as he had opportunity. At one time we find him in Northampton, standing where Doddridge stood twenty-five years before, pleading the claims of that gospel whose sweetness and richness so filled his life and so fitted him for death. Then he is at Olney, where no meeting-house could contain the thronging multitude; then among the fashion of Richmond, "expecting much persecution;" and on a Tuesday, at the Tabernacle in London, attending a "general sacrament, lasting from six till ten, where, blessed be God, thousands communicated."

Now we follow him to Wales and stop with him some bright morning on the road, where he preaches, at "the blessed consecration of an old barn, on preparing 'a habitation for the Lord.'" Rowland loves the hearty tone of Welsh piety, it is "savoury and well baked," and he is received with open arms; he preaches three or four sermons a day, never less than an hour long, and the people follow him by thousands. Another Whitefield is ranging over the hills, another Howell Harris is revisiting the beloved preaching spots and reviving the hearts of God's dear people. No inclemency of the weather hinders the gathering of the peasantry. Many a time, it is said, did he stand through a heavy shower, preaching to a vast concourse of these hardy men, who seemed unconscious of the rain, and were as orderly and attentive as if sunshine were overhead. No fair weather hearers these; and he used afterwards to say to his London audience, when the weather had kept them at home on the Sabbath, "Ah, if you loved the gospel as the Welsh do, you would not mind a shower."

These labours, abundant and blessed as there is reason to believe they were by the great Bishop of souls, vexed those in authority, and prevented his further advancement in the church; he never was ordained priest, and the disappointment is only thus briefly recorded: "Missing of full orders, I thought it was my duty again to begin my public labours as usual." The friendship of the church authorities could give no additional value to his labours, nor could its displeasure rob them of their power.

The Tabernacle and Tottenham Court chapel hailed Rowland Hill as a successor of Whitefield, and crowds attended on his preaching.

In the early part of his career, while under the paternal frown, Lady Huntingdon had received the ardent and self-forgetting young man with an open heart, and gave him a cordial welcome beneath her roof. Subsequently a coolness seems to have sprung up between them: though mutually respecting each other, and mutually wishing each other God speed in *separate* paths of usefulness, they do not appear to have wrought harmoniously together.

The committee of Spa Fields chapel, anxious at one time to secure his services for that portion of London, consulted Lady Huntingdon in reference to inviting him to supply the pulpit. In reply to the letter addressed to her on the subject, she said, with the distinctness which always marked her movements, "Without reserve to you, my kind friend, and with every best wish to dear Mr Venn, Mr Hill cannot preach for me. This must not be pressed. Should any future day prove it expedient, it may be considered; but be assured it cannot be now. Mr Piercy will be succeeded at Spa Fields by Mr Philips, the master of the college, till some other of our ministers return from their four quarterly excursions around the kingdom. He is a gracious, worthy, and faithful minister; he is not only sufficiently judicious for a critic to hear, but welcome to every heart that loves the Lord. Respected Christian love to you and dear Mr Venn, and to the committee."

Her conduct in reference to the young man, was like the language of the patriarch of old to his kinsman Lot, "Let there be no strife, I pray thee, betwixt me and thee; for we be brethren. Is not the whole land before thee? Separate thyself, I pray thee, from me." Would not much discontent and discord be nipped in the bud, and the people of God be saved from much just reproach, if they whose strong individualities or peculiar opinions cannot harmonise, would kindly part, seeking distinct fields of labour, "one to the right, and the other to the left; for is not the whole land before us?"

Rowland is perhaps now at London, dwelling at the Tabernacle parsonage, and helping to form a society for the purpose of enabling pastors to itinerate in their immediate districts, after the example of Berridge and Grimshaw; this association received the name of *Societas Evangelica,* or what with us would be more familiarly termed a home missionary society. Or perhaps he is at Wotton, the place which he called home after his marriage, a beautiful town a hundred miles north-west of London, commanding a fine prospect of the Welsh mountains and the silvery Severn, with woody knolls and green dales, and all the rich variety of an English landscape on every side. Here, in a picturesque situation, he built a house, with a chapel called The Tabernacle, which Robert Hall pronounces "one of the most paradisiacal spots he was ever in." But Mr Hill's friends became anxious, at last, to secure his permanent services in the great metropolis; accordingly a subscription was set on foot for the purpose of erecting a chapel at St George's Fields, the scene of former conquests, and a region whose spiritual barrenness loudly appealed to the friends of humanity.

"I am persuaded your ladyship will rejoice," wrote Berridge to Lady Huntingdon, who was then at Trevecca, "that dear Rowley is going, with the Lord's help, to erect a standard for the gospel in the very middle of the devil's dominions in London. What a bellowing and clamour the old enemy will make, at this fresh invasion of his kingdom. But he may storm and rage and persecute, Christ's cause must and will prevail over all opposition. A meeting has been held, and I am told the place fixed upon is one of the worst spots in London. This much is satisfactory. Fine soil for ploughing and sowing! By and by, my lady, we shall hear of the reaping time, the harvest, and the harvest-home. How glorious will be the triumphs of the gospel in that place. Some of the blessed fruits we may expect to meet in our Father's kingdom above. I need not remind your dear ladyship to pour forth a volley of prayers for the success of this sanctuary."

"Such," the countess tells us, "is the very reviving news from London. I, who have known Mr Hill from his first setting out, can testify, that no man ever engaged with more heart-felt earnestness in bringing captives from Satan to the glorious liberty of the gospel; and it will require all the energies of his zealous and enterprising spirit to erect the standard of the Cross in that part of London, where ignorance and depravity prevail to an awful degree. Though I have seen sufficient cause to exclude him from my chapel for the present, yet I cordially rejoice in the success which has attended his faithful labours. I knew him when a youth at the university, when persecuted by his family, when in pecuniary distress; and he was as a son to me, received into my house, and preached for me everywhere. My heart's desire and prayer to God is, that this undertaking may prosper most abundantly, and that many souls may there be gathered to the true Shiloh, and be crowns of his rejoicing in the great day."

Not only did the undertaking meet with her cordial approbation, but she aided it by a liberal subscription. The corner-stone of this now well-known house of worship, called Surrey Chapel, situated between Blackfriars bridge and the Obelisk, south of the Thames, was laid, with appropriate services, on the 24th of June, 1782, when a sermon was preached by Mr Hill from *Isaiah 28:16*, "Behold, I lay in Zion for a foundation a stone, a tried stone, a precious corner-stone, a sure foundation." The chapel was vested in the hands of fifteen trustees, its doctrinal basis the articles of the Church of England, and its pulpit free to pious ministers of all denominations and of every country.

"The church turned me off, and not I her," its pastor used to say in later times. "I confess, I like a little more liberty than she allows; and, thank God, I can ask the great Dr Chalmers and great Dr Morrison and others, when they come to London, to preach in Surrey chapel pulpit. I suppose they would not let the Apostle Paul, if he were to come upon earth now, preach in his own cathedral."

Surrey chapel, or Rowland Hill's chapel, as it is frequently called, is an object of great interest to Christian travellers from this side of the Atlantic; and one says of it, "Probably no place of worship has been the source of more institutions for promoting the glory of God and the welfare of men, than this has been;" indeed we find springing up, soon after his settlement, a "School of Industry," a "Benevolent Society for the Relief and Personal Visitation of the Sick Poor," a "Dorcas Association," a society or "Social Meetings" for young converts; social prayer-meetings were gathered here and there, in which he mingled with a cordial and delighted interest; and afterwards he and his church took an active part in founding several of the principal benevolent institutions of the age.

Mr Hill now became a settled pastor and a permanent resident of London, and lover as he was of the picturesque and beautiful in nature, the change of homes would have been painful to one less ardently attached to his heavenly work. The present occupants of Surrey-side can hardly realise, that all about the house he then lived in was a swampy marsh edged with the abodes of vicious poverty.

Yet Mr Hill had his summer tours and haunts, when he revisited the scenes of his early labours, refreshed himself on the green banks of the Severn, and rejoiced in his sylvan retreat at Wotton; indeed, he sometimes humorously subscribes himself, "Rector of Surrey chapel, vicar of Wotton-under-edge, and curate of all the fields, commons, and so on, throughout England and Wales."

His dear old friends Berridge and Venn sometimes supplied the pulpit of the absent pastor, and never was he more gratified than when his people were thus fed with the marrow and fatness of Christian truth. An annual exchange also took place between Mr Hill and Dr Scott, chaplain of the Lock Hospital, "After I had been a few years in London," said the venerable commentator, "I refused to preach irregularly, except as once a year I consented to exchange pulpits with Mr Hill of Surrey chapel, that being the stipulated condition of his preaching a charity-sermon for the hospital."

Rowland Hill, whose life and labours extended more than thirty years into the nineteenth century, and whose fame was almost as much the wonder of our childhood as was Whitefield that of our grand-parents, is a bright ray from that elder time, when Whitefield and Wesley, Berridge and Venn, gemmed with their heavenly radiance a dark night in the history of the church.

19
The Secession

IN SPA FIELDS, or Clerkenwell, as it is now better known, then a northern suburb of London, a large building had been erected called the Parthenon, designed especially for a place of Sunday amusement, where, in its whirlpools of riot and excess, many both of the young and old wrecked their hopes for this world and the next. But in this case, the wages of sins proving low, the building was, after a while, put up for sale or lease, and those who had the spiritual desolations of that part of the metropolis at heart, were anxious to secure it for a place of divine worship. Two awakened clergymen belonging to the establishment had their eyes fixed upon it for this purpose, determining to fit it up at their own expense for that preaching which would seek and save them which are lost. Meanwhile Lady Huntingdon, advised of the sale, immediately saw the importance of the stand, and began to consult with her friends upon the propriety of taking it herself.

Mr Toplady discouraged the movement: the first outlay, he thought, must be large, and the stated outgoings afterwards were calculated at £400 a year; the place was far out of town, and the ways to it none of the best in winter. "And consider also," he adds, "the supply of constant and able ministers which such a chapel would require; where are they to be had?"

Lady Huntingdon yielded to the prudent suggestions of her advisers, though contrary to her wishes and convictions; "for my heart," she tells us, "is strongly set upon having this temple of folly dedicated to Jehovah Jesus, the great Head of his church and people. Dear Mr Berridge does not discourage the undertaking, but says I may count upon a fit of sickness if I engage in this affair. I feel so deeply for the perishing thousands in that part of London, that I am ready to run any risk; and though at this moment I have not a penny to command, yet I am so firmly persuaded of the goodness of the Master whose I am, and whom I desire to serve, that I shall not want gold or silver for the work. It is his cause; he has the hearts of all at his disposal, and I shall have help when he sees fit to employ me in his service. Nevertheless, with some regret, I give up the matter this time; those on the spot may be able to judge better than I can, but *faith* tells me to *go forward*, nothing fearing, nothing doubting."

Lady Huntingdon having relinquished her plans, the building was taken by a company of gentlemen, who converted it into a place of divine worship and engaged two excellent preachers to supply the desk. Thus a faithful and efficient ministry was set up in Spa Fields. The spacious edifice was filled with hearers, while the whole neighbourhood shared in their labours of love; the sick were visited, the sorrowful comforted, and sinners were led to repentance and newness of life.

The zealous and abundant labours of these faithful men soon stirred up the hostility of the minister of St James', the parish church, who, resenting the implied reproach which their earnest ministrations cast upon himself, determined if possible to drive them from the field. He accordingly set up his right to nominate the chaplains and preach in the chapel whenever he pleased; he formally demanded the sacramental money, and all the income derived from the seats or other sources to be paid to him, and on pain of non-compliance threatened to bring the matter before the ecclesiastical courts.

These claims, so subversive of the rights and authority of the proprietors, were firmly resisted; the curate, whose motives inclined him neither to generosity nor justice, exasperated by the dignified stand of the proprietors, commenced a suit against the Spa Fields preachers in the Consistorial court of the Bishop of London.

The offending clergymen were speedily cited to appear before it to answer to the charge of irregularity, in carrying on divine worship in a place not episcopally dedicated, and in opposition to the wishes of the minister of the parish. Verdicts were found against them, and they were ordered to desist from their ministrations; the chapel was closed, and the once flourishing congregation broken up and scattered.

The affair gave great pain to the friends of true religion. As soon as the result was known, Lady Huntingdon hastened to London to see if something could not be done in order to rescue the chapel from the persecuting curate. An opportunity now offered to follow counsels less timid than those formerly given, and more in harmony with her own daring and hopeful spirit. Lord Dartmouth and Mr Thornton advised Lady Huntingdon to become proprietor of the chapel, and thus place it on a footing with her other chapels, under the protection and jurisdiction of a peeress of the realm.

"Blessed be God," she exclaims, "for the ability and strength which has been given me in the prosecution of this affair. O pray that his presence may be with us at the dedication, and the power of his arm revealed in the conversion of sinners to himself. My eye is directed to this ultimate and only end of all my labours."

The house passed into her hands, and was again opened under auspices favourable to true religion. Lady Huntingdon's income at this time was no more than sufficient to meet the already numerous demands made upon it by her various undertakings to extend the Redeemer's kingdom. But her faith and courage never failed. Her vigorous and resolute spirit rose above all timid counsels or temporary policy, in things needful to be done. Once clearly decided in her views of duty, she knew no faltering, and her "must be" carried with it a wonderful power to clear away the hindrances which might stop the progress of less ardent and resolute temperaments.

We note at this time this pleasing incident. A gentleman who assisted her in the management of Spa Fields chapel, called one day at her house to remonstrate with her on the impropriety of taking measures for another chapel in the metropolis, without having the means for carrying them out. Before he left the house her letters arrived. As she opened one, her face brightened and tears came into her eyes. The letter ran thus: "An individual who has heard of Lady Huntingdon's exertions to spread the gospel, requests her acceptance of the enclosed draft." It was for five hundred pounds, the exact sum then required for the purposed undertaking. "Here," said she, "take it, and pay for the chapel; and be no longer faithless, but believing."

As a peeress of the realm, Lady Huntingdon believed she possessed the right of employing her own chaplains when and where she chose on her own premises. In this, however, she was destined to be undeceived; for the curate of St James', with unabated zeal, renewed his attack both upon her chapel and preachers, and once more carried the matter before the tribunals of the church, and here she fared no better than her predecessors. The suit was decided against her; verdicts were issued against Dr Haweis and Mr Glascott, the preachers of Spa Fields, and they were prohibited from again exercising their ministerial functions at the chapel. Harassed by the suit, and surprised at the result, Lady Huntingdon lost no time in consulting the highest legal advice, and submitted the following questions to a leading lawyer at the English bar:

"Is the domestic chapel of a peer of this realm exempt from ecclesiastical jurisdiction, and licensed?

"What constitutes such domestic chapel? Is it sufficient that it be contiguous with the house or usual residence of such peer, and that divine service be performed according to the Church of England, by a regularly ordained minister?

"May such chapel be opened to any besides his immediate domestics, if such peer pleases to admit them?

"Must the clergyman so officiating necessarily be registered in the Commons; or is an appointment under such peer's hand and seal, with or without a pecuniary appointment for his services, necessary to constitute him legally qualified for such ministry?

"If he is cited into the Commons for such exercise of his ministry, can he refuse to appear? Will his plea, as domestic chaplain of such peer, be sufficient bar to further proceedings? Can the case be carried into the King's Bench or House of Lords?

"Is it necessary that such chapel should be registered in the Bishop's court?"

Her inquiries were promptly answered and accompanied by a letter from Mr Glynne, which will be read with interest in these days of light and freedom:

"In the notes to the queries which your ladyship did me the honour to transmit to me," says he, "you will perceive there are great difficulties in your way. Ecclesiastical law, *as it now stands,* is against you in some points which would not be insurmountable, were our bishops differently minded; but I regret to say that the spirit and the temper of too many of our ecclesiastical rulers is very unfavourable to any liberal or tolerant system; so that nothing can be expected of a set of men who seem so determined, on all occasions, to crush the spirit of inquiry, free opinion, and liberty of conscience. I anxiously look for reformation in some matters connected with the established church, to which I am conscientiously attached; and though I may not live to see any great change, yet I am persuaded the time is not far distant, when bishops will deeply lament that persecuting spirit which has driven so many from the church, and which in too many instances is more in accordance with the intolerant spirit of the Romish church, than with the enlightened principles of the Protestant faith."

The spirit of opposition thus fairly let loose against Lady Huntingdon, encouraged by ecclesiastical authority, she saw no end to the litigations which might ensue, bringing a long train of perplexities and expenses which must essentially embarrass her operations and impair her usefulness. Under these circumstances, she cast about in her mind how to free herself from the power which could persecute. Sorrowfully and anxiously, but not long, did she consider the painful subject.

"Should further actions come," she says, "I must patiently endure while power conquers right. In this case I am reduced to turn the finest congregation, not only in England but in any part of the world, into a dissenting meeting, unless by the medium of secession. Our ministers might occupy a neutrality between church and dissent-secession. Such ministers could supply any work that opened, yet not be obnoxious to either party, while by preaching and practice they maintained the doctrines of the Reformation. Little, weak, and insufficient as I account my light among others, this becomes the only noble and honest testimony."

It was not without a struggle that Lady Huntingdon decided to take a step which must not only lay her open to invidious remark and severe censure, but deprive her of the ministerial cooperation of some of her most esteemed friends. The decision of the Consistorial court had indeed already done this, but her proposed course would confirm that decision, and place her, if beyond the control, also beyond the professional services of faithful and true men of the English church. The example and success of Wesley encouraged her; and she felt that a denomination differing from "the Wesleyans in holding the doctrinal articles of the Church of England in their Calvinistic sense – from the Independents, by admitting the lawfulness, and in many cases the expediency of using a scriptural liturgy from the Church of England herself, in being free to adopt whatever they deem valuable in her services, and to refuse what appears to them objectionable, while they are exempt from that corrupting influence to which she is exposed by her union with the state," and yet agreeing with each in the essential doctrines of the gospel, might occupy a most favourable position for those evangelising labours which England then seemed so much to need. And she was the more urged to this on surveying the good already accomplished by her chapels, and beholding what large and destitute fields still opened for the faithful efforts of her students and preachers.

"I am to be cast out of the church now," she says, "only for what I have been doing these forty years – speaking and living for Jesus Christ; and if the days of my captivity are now to be accomplished, those that turn me out, and so set me at liberty, may soon feel what it is by sore distress themselves for these hard services which they have caused me.

"Blessed be the Lord, I have not one care relative to this event, but to be found exactly faithful to God and man through all. I have been severely handled and vilified, but none of these things move me, determined that the short remnant of my life shall be employed in setting up the standard and enlarging the circle of evangelical light and truth."

"Hitherto it had not been generally understood," says her English biographer, "how far the privileges of a peeress of the realm extended; but the trials which took place at the Consistorial court of London respecting Spa Fields chapel, first decided the character of Lady Huntingdon's chapels as dissenting places of worship. Conscientious clergymen at this decision were painfully circumstanced. On the one hand multitudes in every neighbourhood were perishing in ignorance; on the other, the regulations of the established church forbade their stepping over the boundaries of a parish. The result was, that many, though sincerely attached to the Church of England, preferred what seemed to them the lesser evils, and preached beyond the limits of their own parishes, but generally without incurring ecclesiastical penalties. Berridge's caustic reply to the reproof of his diocesan for preaching beyond parish bounds, is well known: 'Why, my lord, I see many parsons playing at bowls and going a hunting out of their parishes, yet they are not rebuked; why should I be blamed more than they?'"

In order to be freed from all further annoyances, two gentlemen of the established church, Messrs. Wills and Taylor, who had been prohibited by the court from preaching in Lady Huntingdon's chapels, determined to secede from the establishment, and taking the oaths of allegiance as dissenting ministers, find shelter under the Toleration Act. Mr Wills was then appointed minister at Spa Fields, and henceforth the worship of God was carried on without molestation. Although misrepresented and misunderstood, their vindication shows them to be men whose candour, common sense, and true catholicity no one could seriously call in question.

"We beg leave," they say to the archbishops and bishops of the Church of England, "with all humility and due respect, to inform your lordships, that we have for some time past been engaged in the service of the chapels belonging to the countess dowager of Huntingdon; apprehending that those places of worship, under the protection of her ladyship as a peeress of the realm, were in no wise contrary to the laws, ecclesiastical and civil.

"But whereas, by a late decision of the Consistorial court of the Bishop of London, it appears that her ladyship cannot authorise us to officiate in her chapels in the public manner wherein we have been accustomed to exercise our ministry, we perceive ourselves – as long as we continue in the established church – reduced to the necessity of knowingly and wilfully opposing the law of that church, whereof we are at present ministers, or of withdrawing our services from the various congregations to whom we have administered for a long season, and trust we have, by the blessing of God, been made useful. But as we cannot take either of these steps with a good conscience, nor submit to those ecclesiastical canons that would prevent the discharge of the ministerial commission we have received from God and man to the fullest extent; and yet desire from principle – as we have invariably done from our ordination – to spread and maintain faithfully the fundamental doctrines contained in the articles, homilies, and liturgy of the Church of England, through the various parts of the kingdom as we have opportunity, we think there is no alternative left but for us to secede or withdraw peaceably from the established church, and under the protection of the Toleration Act, continue to maintain her doctrines, though we cannot in all things submit to her discipline. And this we desire to do, not from a factious or schismatical spirit, not from a design to propagate heresies in the church of God, nor from any sinister or lucrative motives whatsoever; but for a simple view of glorifying God, of preaching the gospel, and of being useful to our fellow-creatures in that way which is most agreeable to our own consciences, and which we humbly conceive to be the most calculated for the general good of those many thousands that attend the ministry of ourselves and of those connected with us."

This manly stand did credit to them as Christian men and ministers of God. The students of Trevecca, no longer being able to obtain episcopal ordination, were henceforth to be ordained on the plan of secession; and on the 9th of March, 1783, the first ordination of ministers in Lady Huntingdon's connection took place in Spa Fields chapel. Six young men from Trevecca were to be set apart to the office of the holy ministry, and the chapel at an early hour was filled to overflowing. A profound solemnity rested upon the large congregation. After the opening supplications and hymns of praise, Mr Taylor reviewed the reasons which had led to a secession, and the motives which influenced himself and his co-worker Mr Wills in detaching themselves from the establishment.

"This Bible, this precious Bible," said the speaker, laying his hand upon the inspired volume, "we take for our rule, and acknowledge it as such in all matters of faith and practice. We have not, we dare not take any other. Believing this book, therefore, to be the only standard, we receive or refuse the sentiments, opinions, and doctrines of every man, as weighed in this balance. And further, believing this pure Word of God, we abjure that heretical tenet which supposes either that the popes of Rome, the bishops of England, or any individual whatever, is the head of Christ's church. This is a prerogative belonging only to Christ himself. Him, therefore, and only him we acknowledge as such."

After intermediate services, the confession of faith already subscribed to by the ordaining clergymen, and to be received by ministers in the connection, was publicly read, which recognised all the distinguishing doctrines of the gospel.

At the laying on of hands, the candidates knelt before the altar and each received from the ordaining clergyman a copy of the Bible, with the injunction, "Take thou authority to preach the Word of God, and to administer his appointed ordinances, in the name of the Father, and of the Son, and of the Holy Ghost." After this, a solemn and impressive charge was given by Mr Wills from the words of Paul to Timothy: "Take heed unto thyself, and to thy doctrines; continue in them: for in doing this thou shalt both save thyself and them that hear thee."

Henceforth the societies of Lady Huntingdon became known as a separate denomination; free in exercising their powers, and untrammelled by ecclesiastical restrictions, but cut off from those who once loved to labour with them and for them. Romaine and Venn no longer officiated in those pulpits once so dear to them, although they still cordially loved the chapels, and maintained an unabated attachment to their founder.

At the time of the secession, the connection numbered sixty-seven chapels, seven only of which were the private property of the countess; and though the control which she exercised over them was not a strictly legal one, yet, originated and aided by her princely munificence, she was, during her lifetime, their natural overseer or head, and her strong powers of mind, united with her knowledge and taste for business, peculiarly fitted her for the oversight of this great work. She kept herself carefully informed of the state of affairs, appointed and removed ministers, directed the labours of students, appointed laymen in each congregation to superintend its secular concerns, indicted letters of advice and admonition, received applications for preachers, conducted a numerous correspondence; in a word, such was her strong personal and moral influence, that no changes were made or plans executed in the connection, without her counsel and approbation.

"Of what church do you profess yourselves?" was asked of Dr Haweis, one of the trustees of Lady Huntingdon's property.

"We desire," he replies, "to be esteemed members of Christ's catholic and apostolic church, and essentially one with the Church of England, of which we regard ourselves as living members. And though, as the Church of England is now governed, we are driven to a mode of ordaining ministers and maintaining societies not amenable to what we think to be abused episcopal jurisdiction, yet our mode of governing and regulating our congregations will probably be allowed to be essentially episcopal. With us a few preside. The doctrines we subscribe to are those of the Church of England, in the literal and grammatical sense. Nor is the liturgy of the church performed more devoutly, or the Scriptures better read for the edifying of the people, by any congregations in the realm, than by those in our connection."

20
Harvest Home

LADY HUNTINGDON had now gone beyond threescore years and ten, with no abatement of her labours, or of the vigour and resoluteness which distinguished her character. She knew indeed neither weariness nor rest. The new divine life with which she arose from her sick-bed in the days of her youth and splendour, was subject to none of the infirmities of the natural body; and far beyond the common life of man, it seemed to lift her above the weakness of the flesh, and clothe decaying nature with the strength and beauty of an immortal vesture. Lady Anne Erskine was her constant companion, devoted to her interests, animated by the same lofty purposes, and willing both to suffer and rejoice with her.

In 1789, the venerable countess was called to mourn the death of her eldest son, Lord Huntingdon, nor was this the only occasion when her heart had bled on account of him. He was an elegant and accomplished man, and had filled several offices of trust and honour under his sovereign; but strongly tinctured with the profligacy and practical infidelity of the times, he neither understood the excellency of his mother's principles in life, nor their saving power in death. Mr Grimshaw had many conversations with the young earl, and pronounced the fault not so much in the head as the heart. Wherever it was, he died as he had lived, at the age of sixty years.

During her last years, Lady Huntingdon lived the greater part of the year at her house in Spa Fields, London, next door to the chapel, where her style of living befitted less an English peeress than an heir of glory. Her equipage and furniture were extremely simple; and although her income was much increased at her son's death, so ample were her benefactions that she allowed herself but one dress a year, a degree of economy that might well shame many a Christian woman whose adorning consists far more in the "putting on of apparel," than "the hidden man of the heart in that which is not corruptible."

"I remember," said one, "calling on her with a person who came from the country: when we came out he turned his eye towards the house, and after a short pause exclaimed, 'What a lesson! Can a person of her noble birth, nursed in the lap of grandeur, live in such a house, so meanly furnished? and shall I, a tradesman, be surrounded with luxury and elegance? From this moment I shall hate my house, my furniture, and myself for spending so little for God, and so much in folly.'"

"With an income of only twelve hundred pounds a year, spent in the service of God, what wonders was she able to perform," exclaims one of her friends. "She maintained the college at her own expense, she erected chapels in most parts of the kingdom, and she supported preachers who were sent to preach in various parts of the world. This was indeed consecration to God. Go thou, therefore, who art saying, 'What shall I render unto the Lord for all his benefits?' and do likewise.

"Thou canst not evidence thy love to God or man by adding house to house and field to field, or by treasuring up thy riches behind the exchange. On the contrary, if God hath given thee wealth with a liberal hand, and thou hast no heart to expend it in his service, it will convince every being but thyself that thou hast no love to him, and that thy professions are not thy principles."

In approaching her eighty-fourth year, Lady Huntingdon felt that her work was nearly done; the infirmities of age came upon her, and the once robust and active frame, so alert to do the bidding of its spiritual tenant, began to ask for indulgence and to crave rest. Her business was carefully arranged, her extensive charities all provided for, responsible persons had been selected to carry out her plans, and though still diligent with the business of the evening, she looked forward with "strong immortal hope" to the dawn of that tomorrow whose glorious sun would have no setting.

As she sits in her elbow-chair, and memory runs back over the long past, and through this brilliant period of the history of the church signalised by so many triumphs and trophies, is there no whisper of self-gratulation for the conspicuous part which she bore, the friend and helper of God's chosen ones, the leader and counsellor of many of his people?

"O, who would dare to produce the best works of his best days before God for their own sake?" she exclaims; "Sufficiently blessed and secure are we, if we can but cry, 'God be merciful unto me a sinner.' Let me be found 'accepted in the Beloved.'"

"Drawing near to him," she said on another occasion, "what hope could I entertain, if I did not know the efficacy of his blood? How little could anything of mine give a moment's rest to the departing soul – so much sin and self mixing with the best, and always so short of what I owe."

Coming from her chamber one morning, and taking her place in the easy-chair, an unwonted light was spread over her countenance. "The Lord hath been present with my spirit this morning in a remarkable way," she soon said; "What he means to convey to my mind I know not; it may be my approaching departure: my soul is filled with glory. I am as in the element of heaven itself." Only a few days after this she ruptured a blood-vessel, from which she never recovered. "How do you feel?" asked Lady Anne, who sat at the bedside of her friend. "I am well; all is well, well for ever," was the triumphant answer of this aged believer. "I see, wherever I turn my eyes, whether I live or die, nothing but victory." What was there in the weakness and suffering of decaying nature to dictate a reply like this?

Her sickness commenced in November; the silver cord was gently loosed, for she lingered through the winter until June. By the ministry of sickness she grew patient and childlike, and often said, "I am cradled in the arms of love and mercy;" and again, when it seemed a great way to the better land, she "longed to be at home." "My work is done; I have nothing to do but to go to my Father;" and a few hours before the last struggle she whispered joyfully, "I shall go to my Father tonight;" and so she went home, June 17, 1791. Her age was eighty-four. She was buried in the family tomb at Ashby de la Zouch, and her name is with the Miriams, the Marys, and the Marthas of the church of God.

Berridge, Romaine, and Venn, all in the evening of their days, still lingered on the earthly scene. It was during this year that the rector of Yelling came to preach in London for the last time, and he says, "I took my final leave of Surrey chapel, addressing myself to a great multitude from *Hebrews 10:23:* 'Let us hold fast the profession of our faith without wavering; for He is faithful that promised.' My work is nearly ended."

Soon after, accompanied by two of his children, he paid a visit to the venerable pastor of Everton, "dear brother Berridge, whose sight," he tells us, "is very dim, his ears can scarcely hear, and his faculties are fast decaying; but in this ruin of the earthly tabernacle, it is refreshing," adds his friend, "to see the joy in his countenance and the lively hope with which he looks for the day of his dissolution. In his prayer with me and my children, we were much affected by his commending himself to the Lord as if quite alone, not being able to read, or hear, or do anything; 'but I have, Lord,' said he, 'thy presence and thy love; *that* sufficeth.'"

Mr Berridge's large fortune seems to have been far spent towards the close of his life, for we find Romaine in London begging on his behalf for "the support of two preachers and their horses, for several local preachers, and the rent of some barns for them to preach in;" so that he strove to keep his under-shepherds still in the field. Nor did he himself ever relinquish his work; for we find him making his yearly visits to the metropolis while life lasted, and with tottering steps climbing up the pulpit stairs of the Tabernacle and Surrey chapel, revered for the sturdy godliness of his character, and pointed out to strangers for the quaint sayings and eccentric doings which had been noised about concerning him throughout the kingdom. He was expected in London to preach, when tidings came of his death in 1793, aged seventy-six.

Let us go to Blackfriars or St Dunstan's and once more see Romaine, although there is said to be little left in his sermons but heaven, and the doctrines which he so long preached as *truths,* he now finds in a deep and rich experience to be *blessings* indeed. He is a cheerful, pleasant old man. Like a newly-found diamond, he was once rough, very sharp, and of great point, but the discipline of many years has polished the hard exterior, and brought forth its hidden lustre; his virtues shine with a soft and serene beauty. His summer and winter campaigns Romaine kept up, like a brave old soldier, to the last; during the winter remaining at his post in London, and in summer visiting the towns and villages which were the scenes of his early conquests, and now rich with the trophies of his zeal and faithfulness.

The last year of his life his strength gradually began to fail, and when people met and asked him how he was, his usual answer was, "As well as I can be out of heaven;" and at the close of a seven weeks' illness, the last words which lingered on his bloodless lips were, "Holy, holy, holy, blessed Jesus, to thee be endless praise!" He died in 1795, aged eighty-one.

Venn is now writing, "I am so infirm as not to be able to pray with my own family; nevertheless, 'He that loved me will love me to the end;'" and then, with an ever-thoughtful tenderness for others, he says, "One thing only I desire without ceasing, that for the sake of the thousands to whom I have preached the unsearchable riches of Christ, I may in the hour of death look through an opened heaven to a crucified Saviour smiling upon a poor guilty soul." His wife died a year before him, and all his children having married except Kitty, who remained his nurse and devoted companion, he left the rectory of Yelling and came to Clapham, where his son was rector, and dwelt with him. It is said that the near prospect of dissolution so elated his mind that it proved a stimulus to life. On one occasion Mr Venn, observing some fatal symptoms, said, "Surely these are good." "Sir," answered the physician, "in this state of joyous excitement you cannot die." Nor will he die; he yet liveth and speaketh, though he passed from the earthly scene in 1797, at the age of seventy-three, and entered upon those joys, blessed foretastes of which cheered, comforted, nay, in moments often transported his soul, in its pilgrimage below.

Standing as we are at the bed of death, in the glowing language of the lyric shall we not exclaim,

> *"How glorious is the gift of faith,*
> *That cheers the darksome tomb,*
> *And through the damp and gloomy grave*
> *Can shed a rich perfume.*
>
> *"Triumphant faith! it lifts the soul*
> *Above desponding fears;*
> *Exults in hope of heaven her home,*
> *And longs to enter there."*

Who is not ready to put up the heartfelt petition, "May my last days be like theirs"? Are you as ready to flee from the wrath to come; as ready to embrace the offers of mercy through a crucified

Redeemer; as ready to lay hold on eternal life? The triumphs of faith are for those who lead a believer's life.

In her will, Lady Huntingdon devised her chapels, houses, furniture, and all the residue of her estates and effects, to four trustees, Dr Haweis and his wife, Lady Anne Erskine, and Mr Lloyd, directing them at their death to appoint successors; and in a codicil requesting her children, the Countess of Moira and her husband being the only survivors, to approve and confirm the disposition which had thus been made of her property.

The lease of the college building at Trevecca having nearly expired, measures had been adopted before the countess' death to remove the institution somewhere nearer London; for this purpose a building and lands were taken at Cheshunt, delightfully situated on New river, twelve miles from London. It was reopened on the 24th of August, 1792, the anniversary of its establishment at Trevecca, and of the birthday of its distinguished founder and patroness. In anticipation of her death, and the consequent loss of income from that source, funds had been raised for its future support, and the interests of the college vested in the hands of seven trustees, in whom resides the right of admitting or rejecting students, and the appointment or dismissal of tutors. The students are boarded and educated for four years, entirely at the charge of the college; and according to the liberal principles of the institution, every student is at liberty, at the close of the prescribed course of study, to serve in the ministry of the gospel in any of the churches of the Lord Jesus Christ. Rev Isaac Nicholson of the established church was appointed president.

Dr John Harris, whose *"Great Teacher"* has taught so many on this side of the Atlantic, is now theological professor at Cheshunt.

When it was known what disposition Lady Huntingdon had made of her property, the trustees agreed that as Lady Anne Erskine had long been familiar with the business transactions of the connection, she should be requested still to occupy the house at Spa Fields and carry on the necessary correspondence, and exercise a superintending control – advising with her co-labourers, and rendering an account to them, when required, of the state of affairs.

Lady Anne inherited much of the talent of the Erskine family. At the age of eight years she first felt the strivings of the Holy Spirit, and though her early life was passed amid the fashionable follies of her rank and day, an acquaintance with the Hills of Hawkstone revived her religious feelings, and led her to a serious consideration of eternal things. At Bath she met Lady Huntingdon, whose conversation and example instructed and confirmed her faith; she turned from the pomps and vanities of the world, and made an unreserved dedication of herself to the service of her Lord. Congenial in their purposes and principles, Lady Anne was taken to the countess' heart, and invited to her home, where she found scope for that activity of mind which could not rest satisfied without its appropriate work to do.

"During the twelve years after her active life commenced," runs a brief account of her, "she was indefatigably employed in the work of God. Her correspondence was very extensive. Her room was hardly without visitors from morning till night, giving an account of commissions fulfilled, or taking directions where to go and what to do. She improved every opportunity of conversing with the friends who visited her, especially the young. Indeed, her whole time and thoughts seemed to be engaged to fill up her place, feeling it her delight, as well as her duty, to discharge her trust, as she must answer to the great Shepherd and Bishop of souls."

At Lady Huntingdon's death, her income was reduced to a mere pittance; but she knew in whom she trusted, and many a time was her faith encouraged by receiving supplies in ways most unexpected and for times of the greatest need. One day a lady, on leaving, put a letter on her table, which Lady Anne sent back, supposing it left by mistake. The lady begged her to keep it, and on opening it she found five notes of one hundred pounds each. "A fortune has been left me," said the lady, "and I desire to honour the Lord with my substance and the first-fruits of my increase. I give it to you to strengthen your hands in the cause of God."

"I had not," said Lady Anne, "a shilling in the house at the time. Application had been made to me to receive a chapel into the connection, which I was obliged to refuse; but as soon as I received this money, I sent for the parties and gave it the required aid."

Lady Anne survived her friend twelve years, and after some weeks of slight indisposition, was found one morning sleeping in Jesus.

From an English standpoint shall we not take one backward glance over the stirring scenes just closing around us?

"Whether the chapels in Lady Huntingdon's connection are at this time few or many," says Isaac Taylor in his late admirable work on Methodism, "is a matter of no general moment to inquire; for whether few or many, the connection has subsided into its place as one among the religious communities that hold orthodoxy and evangelical doctrine; and probably it is efficient in a full proportion to its statistics. But with this we have here no concern. What does concern us, is the fact that much that has become characteristic of evangelical Christianity at the present time, had its origin in Lady Huntingdon's drawing-room, that is to say, in the circle of which she was the centre, and her house the gathering point. In a diffusive or undefined manner this religious style has pervaded all religious communions; but within the Episcopal church the transmission was more determinate, and more sharply outlined, and it may there be traced with more precision, and is pregnant with further consequences.

"In fact, this religious transmission, which connects the venerated names of Venn, Newton, Scott, Milner, and others in no very remote manner with the founders of Methodism, might seem too conspicuous to be called in question: nor does it very clearly appear what those manly and Christian-like feelings are, which would prompt any parties to repudiate it.

"It is the Episcopal church which has inherited the main part of the religious animation and refreshment which has come down from that band of ordained ministers of which we are speaking. Besides those already named, and who stand so nearly related to the present times, in ascending a few years we reach, without a break, that company of men, less regular in their ministrations, but not less deserving of affectionate regard, whose names can by no means be disconnected with Methodism – names which, so long as the church retains her articles and homilies, it would be treason to disown. Let Fletcher lead the way, and let there come Hervey, Grimshaw, Berridge, Romaine, Toplady, Walker, and Shirley.

"It may be granted, that the rise of Methodism brings to view many instances of what may be called independent origination; and it is true, that the minds of men who were unknown to each other, became about the same time similarly affected towards the first truths of the Christian system; so that, when accident or sympathy had brought them into contact, they readily coalesced, and thenceforward thought it their duty and happiness to act in concert. So acting and, so associating, Lady Huntingdon gathered them around herself; and she aided, and to some extent, she directed their movements.

"As with Wesley, so with Lady Huntingdon, a formal separation from the established church was, in each act and instance, submitted to with extreme reluctance, and not until it was felt to be inevitable. When at length the irregularities of the awakened clergy could no longer be winked at by the church authorities, the greater number of them fell back in their places as parish ministers; and this defection, while it gave rise necessarily to a new order of ministers in the 'connection,' whose ordination placed them on a level only with the dissenting ministry, it took place at a time when no alternative was left to Lady Huntingdon's congregations, but to seek protection under the Toleration Act as dissenters.

"Lady Huntingdon was always the object of a warm personal affection with those who were nearest to her. With them, it was always 'our *dear* Lady Huntingdon;' and putting out of view formal eulogies, it is unquestionable, that if she governed her connection as having a right to rule it, her style and behaviour, like Wesley's, indicated the purest motives, and the most entire simplicity of purpose. This, in truth, may be said to be a common characteristic of the founders of Methodism: a devotedness to the service of the Saviour Christ, which none who saw or conversed with them could question.

"The same praise and in the same degree is undoubtedly the due of many of those who were the associates and colleagues of these principal persons. It is as bright a company that we have before us, as we find anywhere on the page of Christian history."

One of the most interesting aspects of this great awakening, to us, is the family likeness which exists among the true children of God; and this is one of the old truths which sometimes break upon us with new favour and beauty, and which we indeed often need to be reminded of. In our company have been Dissenters, Episcopalians, Congregationalists, Methodists, Arminians, Calvinists, by various names are they known among men, yet all bearing the image of their common Lord, and possessing the characteristics which mark them a "peculiar people," the true "Israel of God." Here all that was subordinate and local was set aside, all inferior considerations were swallowed up in the one grand and absorbing object, to live in and to labour for their Redeemer and Lord, Jesus Christ. "I am the Lord's," was the animating principle of their lives, not only lifting them above the ordinary discouragements and indulgences of life, but carrying them through labours and self-denial and opposition, in the pursuit of a spiritual and unseen good, with a steadfastness of purpose that never faltered, and a zeal that knew no abatement. And it not only endowed them with the spirit of conquest, it imbued them also with all the spirit of love, a true, hearty, cordial, self-forgetting love, for one another – a love which knew no sect, demanded no certificates, and was bounded by no state lines. By *this,* might it have been emphatically said, did all men recognise the Lord's disciples, in that they "loved one another." The Old World and the New felt the fraternal tie, and "kissed each other."

When shall the Lord's people again live this fresh and glorious life? When shall the cloven tongues of another Pentecost speak the wonderful works of God? Shall not our hearts' desire and prayer to God be for a new baptism of the Holy Ghost?